MY NAME IS
LOVE

WE'RE NOT ALL THAT DIFFERENT

TROY HADEED

Vatula Publishing

Cover Design: Laura Duffy
Front Cover Photo: Laura Stevens
Back Cover Photo: Sam Jackson – Stories told, by Sam
Interior Design: Rachel Valliere

My Name is Love 275/hardcover – 978-976-97127-0-6
My Name is Love 275/paperback – 978-976-97127-1-3
My Name is Love 275/ebook – 978-976-97127-2-0

DEDICATION

This book is dedicated to anyone who has not had the privilege of knowing love, and also to those who have felt alone, forgotten, or without a sense of community, belonging, or purpose.

The words of this book are in honour of those who struggle to overcome pain, heartbreak, and despair; who, even if just for a moment, struggle to make sense of the human experience.

Lastly, this book is for God, the God that lives in me, the God that lives in you, and the God that will never allow us to forget who we truly are.

CONTENTS

Contents

INTRODUCTION

My father named me after an Irish-bred and English-trained champion thoroughbred racehorse called Troy, and that's my picture on the cover.

The day it was taken, I had just finished guiding twenty-two amazing individuals through sixteen days of intensive yoga-teacher training. We're talking fourteen-hour days, 5 a.m. wake-ups, a demanding schedule, and a whirlwind of emotions and realizations. It was raw, real, rattled our egos, and left no heart untouched.

On the final day, after our last meal and emotional goodbyes, Laura Stevens asked if she could take my portrait. Laura was like family. She had been practising yoga with us online for over two years, and had come from France to embark on the transformational journey. I knew Laura was a photographer by trade, but I hadn't seen her work and wasn't aware of her recognized success in the photography world.

I was exhausted and barely hanging on, but there was no way I was going to let Laura down. I imagined that I was doing her a favour: she would get some shots for her portfolio, and I would get some photos I could use for marketing. I didn't think it would take much more than an hour, because there was no hair or make-up, no lights, no wardrobe, and no production assistant. My skin was salty, I smelt of the ocean, and wore my favourite coffee-stained grey tee-shirt.

About five minutes into our shoot, after a few scattered laughs, genuine smiles, and roughly about ten clicks of her camera, Laura says, "Ok, we're good. I got it."

A week later I looked into this photo and felt like I was being introduced to a part of myself I had never met before. I saw a stillness, a humility, and an absolute emptiness that dissolved any sense of who I thought I was. An emptiness that had nothing to lose and left room for only one thing: love. That photo is a portrait of love, and this book isn't about Troy Hadeed. This book is about love, and how we can get ourselves out of the way so it can come through us.

Our world today breeds an obsession with individuality and identity. It is ingrained in us from birth and constantly reinforced via social culture, subtle messaging, and accepted norms. We identify with and define ourselves by opinions, ideology, lifestyle, sexual orientation, career, nationality, class, race, and everything that revolves around our physical form and name.

The reality is that anything surrounding our current physical body is temporary, and therefore cannot actually define who we are. These ideas of ourselves may give us a sense of belonging and importance, but also create a sense of separateness and difference. I have come to the realization that the only thing I can ever truly identify with is love. I'm not talking about a romantic, superficial, flowery, pastel-coloured love; this love is compassionately fierce, courageous, and confrontational. It is a love that knows no limits or conditions, cannot be put into a box, and excludes no one. To understand and embody this love we must first be willing to lose ourselves and surrender our sense of individual identity.

The journey involves constant introspection, questioning, and a willingness to look into our own conditioning, patterns, flaws, and darkness to see where we can do better.

In this book I share a little of my journey with you and offer some of the perspectives and reflections that I've connected with along the way. I have not figured it out, I am not always able to embody the love I speak of, and there is still lots of conditioning lying ahead of me to navigate. I am not your guru, nor do I want to be. However, if we have the courage to ask the right questions I do believe that the reflections and stories in this book help point us in the direction of love.

Along the journey I've travelled the world by ship; walked coast to coast across Central America; opened a hemp store (not a head shop); became a student and teacher of yoga; birthed a thriving yoga community; founded and sold a biofuel business; spoken with hummingbirds; and embraced silence. I have loved deeply and have been heartbroken. I have been overconfident, humbled, and ashamed. I have trusted wholeheartedly, and I have been wronged. I have also been the heartbreaker, the wrongdoer, and the betrayer of trust. I have drunk of God's nectar and have also danced with the demons of my mind.

We are constantly seeking insight, revelations, and epiphanies that make sense of it all. We look everywhere, we ask teachers and friends, turn to books and music, immerse ourselves in nature, and seek the guidance of elders and gurus. We even travel the world to faraway lands of ashrams and solitude to be told we are gifted and unique. Occasionally we find inspiration, answers that suffice momentarily, or teachings and quotes that are great to share on our social media feeds. Sometimes we have transformative experiences that shift our understanding and open our eyes to new perspectives or lifestyles but still leave us longing for something more.

The understanding, wisdom, and knowledge that satisfy our spiritual longing and quest for answers are not in this book. They are deeply ingrained within your individual and unique journey through the human experience. To find them you must search the depths of your soul, quiet your mind, and tune into the whisper of your heart.

This is a personal journey that requires authenticity, self-inquiry, and the readiness to be accountable. It will sometimes be uncomfortable and feel defeating, but it is the only way to quench that longing for more. The human experience itself is your teacher, everyone who crosses your path is part of the curriculum, and while others may guide you, you are your only guru.

My Name Is Love, on the surface, is a collection of personal reflections, insights, and revelations threaded with some of my real-life experiences. I trust these offerings will inspire you and influence the way you navigate your human experience; but they may also trigger you, challenge you, and shake the very foundation of all you thought to be true. However, if you create the space to see how and where these reflections apply to your life, they expose infinite possibilities to dissolve your conditioning and reveal your true potential to understand and embody love.

> The human experience itself is your teacher, everyone who crosses your path is part of the curriculum, and while others may guide you, you are your only guru.

As you navigate these pages, be cautious of previous filters, narratives, and projections. It's essential to be open, honest, and authentic in your introspection. Focus on how these insights and perspectives apply to your life rather than how they don't. Very often, the things we dismiss are the things we unconsciously wish to avoid, and the subtle desire to reinforce our previous perspectives can blind us to valuable insight.

The struggle to overcome my conditioning is ongoing; but in order to embody the philosophy, teachings, and love presented in this book, I must at least try. I feel we must all at least try.

You can call me Troy, but that is not what I identify with. I am love, and we aren't all that different.

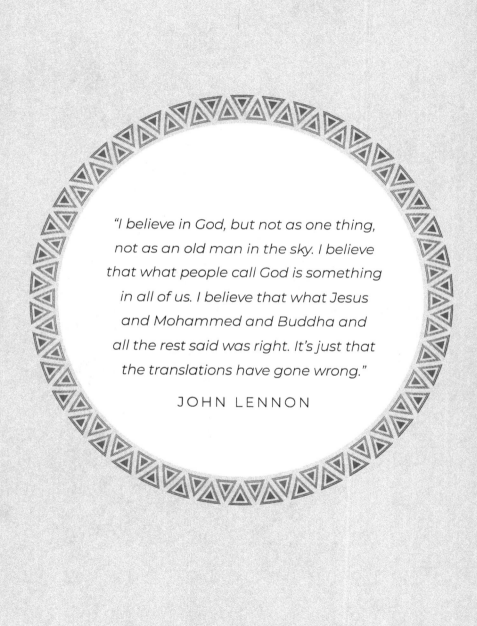

"I believe in God, but not as one thing, not as an old man in the sky. I believe that what people call God is something in all of us. I believe that what Jesus and Mohammed and Buddha and all the rest said was right. It's just that the translations have gone wrong."

JOHN LENNON

Redefining God

I want to begin with God, a topic often charged with so much emotion that many people avoid it like the plague. I love God, and think God is everywhere. Who or whatever God is lives in everything and everyone. Throughout history, God's love has often been presented to us as exclusive rather than inclusive.

While this is not a religious book, I will mention God from time to time, and feel it is necessary to confront the situation head-on, offering a more expansive approach to God.

When I talk about God, I am not referring to a God that belongs exclusively to any religion; religions belong to God. The ideas presented in this chapter may rattle your existing belief system, but please understand that I have no intention of criticizing any organized religion or system of beliefs. My intention here is to share my journey and relationship with God in the hope that it might inspire yours. God has always been a big part of my life, but the closer I came to God, the less I allowed anyone else to define what or who God was for me.

It always gets my attention when I hear someone say, "I don't believe in God. I am an atheist." This statement confused me for many years, and I just couldn't wrap my head around it. With all we experience, how could anyone not believe there was a divine intelligence behind it all? I recognize there is much suffering, hardship, and disconnect in our world. I get that it's difficult to see how God can exist amid such despair. But I also know that within suffering lies the possibility of transformation, growth, and evolution of the spirit. We will discuss this in later chapters, but for now, let's talk about God and the resistance some of us have to the idea of God, more specifically, to the word "God". Furthermore, for those of us who feel we already have a relationship with God, is it our own, or was it one we inherited, and are we allowing space for others to define their personal relationship to God?

Early Intuition

Growing up in a Catholic home, God and spirit were always a big part of my life. I was raised by a saint I call Mom, and to this day, I have a relationship with Christ that I treasure above all. From a young age, however, I couldn't help but feel that so much was being misunderstood through the perspective of "religion". I felt I had an intimate friendship with God, but much of what I was being taught at school and in my community didn't align with what I knew to be true. I could not accept that any one particular group or religion was favoured by God or that God hinged his unconditional love on our obedience. I often questioned how unconditional, infinite, and inclusive love could coexist with eternal punishment. Why were we told to leave all judgement to God, but then taught that some people are "unworthy" of God's love? I prayed, went to confession, and attended church every Sunday. I remember on several occasions listening to sermons and thinking to myself, "This guy doesn't get it." The more my relationship with God deepened, the less I could accept the extent of misinformation and misrepresentation being shared. As I approached adolescence, I began to connect even more to the teachings of Christ, but this time beyond the confines of organized religion.

I came to understand the love of Christ as absolutely limitless and inclusive of everyone, regardless of their religion or even their wrongs and mistakes. Rather than being doomed to the life of a sinner, I felt Christ was calling us to step up and recognize the God that lived within each of us. He even said that we were capable of doing far greater things than he did. As I've grown into adulthood, I have chosen to believe that this was not simply a poetic statement to inspire the masses, but a literal call to embody the love and greatness he came to teach.

I can put my finger on two significant catalysts that deepened my connection to Spirit in ways I could not anticipate. There was my immersion in the raw undeniable intelligence of nature, coupled with a growing intimacy in my yoga practice; an intimacy that brought me to understand my yoga practice as a prayer and quality time with God. But before you shake your head and mutter, "Not another hippie yoga junkie with his head in the clouds!" let me explain.

There are many stereotypical or preconceived ideas about yoga, and I understand why someone might raise an eyebrow at the thought that yoga could deepen my relationship with God. Not only are there many different approaches to the practice, but it has been layered with religious understandings, adopted by the world of health and fitness, and has even found itself being manipulated by Western capitalism. In reality, at its core, yoga is the practice of using the concentrated focus of breath to quiet the mind, induce states of stillness, and ultimately facilitate intimacy with God.

Looking back, I realize my yoga practice cultivated within me the ability to be still and listen. It created a space where I could dial into and be receptive to an internal voice; a very clear intuition that led me to the majestic, forested mountainside of Trinidad's north coast and told me that it would be my home. I was going to be called to see the world differently; but I had to be ready.

Coming to Know God

Coming from a well-to-do neighbourhood, no one would ever have expected me to pack my bags and go live in the forest voluntarily. While I often spent time in nature, I would not have called myself a "bushman" by any means; there were limits to my survival skills. Maybe a naturalist of sorts, but not a bushman.

When I purchased an acre of land in an upcoming eco-development with no existing houses or neighbours, I had no intention of living there anytime soon. I figured by the time I could afford to build a home, the area would surely be more developed. Until then, the plan was to erect a little shack, hang out with friends on the weekends, and make it my getaway. Apparently, though, there was a bigger plan in the works.

About six months later, on that parcel of land, surrounded by nothing but forest, stood my glorified shack, a two-storey board house with a sliding roof. The only doors and walls were the ones that separated the bedroom from the animals of the forest, and even that didn't always work out as planned. While it was not technically a treehouse, it hung under the lush green rainforest canopy on the side of a mountain, so – naturally – it felt like a treehouse. It was nothing more than the desire for adventure and the need to prove myself that drove me to sleep there for the first time. I had no idea that night would change my life.

On that forest mountainside with no human in earshot, I was alone, or so I thought. But aside from the snakes, scorpions, monkeys, and our local folklore spirits, there was something else I couldn't put my finger on. The sunset was spectacular, and as the night sky moved in, the temperature fell, and a distinct shift in the symphony of sounds enveloped me. What was somewhat unfamiliar and uncomfortable became an absolute test of faith. The light that hung above my hammock attracted these erratic tornado-shaped flying insects that behaved like suicide bombers. They were everywhere and had one goal in mind: to take me out. I managed to climb out of my hammock to turn the light out and quickly jumped back into the cocoon. I could feel the tension in my body and the shallowness of my heartbeat as my mind fabricated countless narratives about everything that could go wrong. I thought about my apartment, only thirty minutes away in the suburbs, and acknowledged there would be no shame in getting into my truck and heading for a world of comfort. However, I knew that was not an option, because my mind might have rested easier, but my heart would never have let it go.

Instead, I decided to call on God for backup. Not as one would do in traditional prayer, but as an authentic heart-to-heart one might have with a teacher, a guardian, or even a lover. With my focus on God, one intimate breath after another, my mind began to settle. It wasn't long before my fears subsided, and I slowly opened my eyes to a new reality. As my eyes adjusted to the darkness, the star-scattered night sky revealed itself, and for the first time that night, I noticed moonlight glistening on the leaves of trees like diamonds. Giant rooted soldiers were dancing in the wind hundreds of feet above my head, and a nocturnal orchestra of animals played their tune to the magical twinkle of fireflies. Until that moment, I had been so focused on the threat of darkness that it was all I could experience. In reality, I was the threat. I was the outsider who viewed myself as separate from everything else around me. I had created a scenario where man and nature were battling for survival, rather than one in which I was part of the collective natural magic. A sense of awe and belonging came over every cell of my body, and at that moment, I bore witness to an intelligence that was in absolutely everything. The very same intelligence within me, the same intelligence I recognized as God.

That night God permeated every cell of my body and permanently moved from a concept in my mind to take up residence in my heart. That night I felt God as a formless intelligence that was not governed by human ideas of separateness. In the simplest and most profound way, I discovered that God even lives in what might first appear as darkness. That was the night I felt God without any social or historical filters, boundaries, separation, or fears of judgement.

The following day I moved into the treehouse and called it home for another six years. Eventually the weather took its toll and the treehouse was deemed unsafe, so I had to build a new house on that plot of land, but that mountainside has been my home ever since. When I look back on it now, the timing was no coincidence. That first night in the treehouse was an initiation, and I had to be ready. It was my yoga practice that allowed me to clear the cobwebs of my mind so that I could connect to God not only within me but in all that surrounded me. I had immersed myself in nature before, I had sat in silence for ten days at a time; but something within me shifted that night. I was invited to dissolve the narratives that painted me as separate from everyone and everything else. That night was merely a glimpse into the divine collective intelligence that we call God, but the experience altered the course of my life. I sat in my hammock that first night, lightly kissed by moonlight, and knew that every decision

I had ever made had led me to that moment. That was no accident; nothing was. Divine intelligence was and is everywhere.

Conversations with an Atheist

I acknowledge the historical wrongs and injustices committed in the name of God, and understand why someone might be an atheist. Furthermore, I respect everyone's right to establish their own beliefs; but still, I have great difficulty understanding how anyone could deny some aspect of divine intelligence. I am certainly not offended by those who view themselves as atheists, and I no longer feel the need to convince them otherwise.

But there was that one time when I tried my best to convince an atheist that God existed.

It was during my senior year, on a study-abroad programme called Semester at Sea. I was twenty-one, navigating the world on a ship with nine hundred students for my final year, and he was my professor. In addition to the excitement of travelling the world on a floating university, I was looking forward to his World Philosophy and Religion course. However, it wasn't more than ten minutes into our very first class that his words caught me a bit off-guard.

"I'll give an A+ to anyone who can prove to me that God exists before the end of the semester. You won't even have to sit an exam or submit a paper."

I was confused. At that time I couldn't understand how it was possible for a professor of world philosophy and religion not to believe in God. How could that be? Regardless, I was elated at the prospect of earning an A+ and proving that God existed, especially to my university professor. I thought to myself, "This guy has no idea who he's dealing with – I just hope he enjoys the last of his days as a non-believer." His name on the cover of our textbook should have indicated the battle ahead, but it only sweetened what I thought would be my inevitable victory.

His name was Brian, and it wasn't long before we were on a first-name basis. He saw the light in my eyes when I spoke about God and felt the passion resonating within me. It was clear to him that I knew God existed, but it became evident that knowing it and proving it were two very different things. Every point I presented, he had heard before and was ready for, with a response that dissolved any weight I thought it carried. While I did pass that course, I failed miserably in my endeavour to prove to my professor that God existed. He did, however, leave me with a few humbling realizations that would only unfold years later. The only way to truly influence someone's beliefs is through understanding their perspective, not by trying to force them through yours.

It was over a decade before I once again attempted to engage an atheist on God, but this time was different. While my relationship with God had grown even stronger, I had become more accepting and understanding of varying views and beliefs. I no longer had that urge to be heard or prove anyone wrong. I developed more interest in understanding different opinions and the situations that might have shaped them, while simply offering alternative considerations. This time the conversation presented itself organically, and there was no air of confrontation, no battlefield, just two friends with open hearts.

> The only way to truly influence someone's beliefs is through understanding their perspective, not by trying to force them through yours.

Andrew was some years younger than I, but in many ways far more knowledgeable. He and his father were both academics whose company I thoroughly enjoyed. We shared meals, laughed, and had a good time, but it was our conversations that always had me wanting more. They often held different perspectives, both from each other and from myself, but would always create a space where everyone could share, offer alternative views and considerations, and be understood.

After years of honest and intriguing conversations, I was surprised one night to discover that Andrew didn't believe in God. We had had many conversations surrounding spirituality, religion, morality, and even our mortality.

As it turned out, Andrew hadn't previously felt safe to share his lack of belief, because he assumed that my understanding of God was conventional and bound to religion. That night, a little more mature, with more experience and tools than I had ten years prior, I was not interested in proving to Andrew that God existed. I just wanted to understand how and why he did not believe in God. We sat, and I listened intently, agreeing with or at least acknowledging everything brought to the table: talk of historical wrongs, injustices, oppression, and inhumane, self-righteous acts that have been committed in the name of God. He appeared a little confused that I agreed so readily with his supporting reasoning, and he realized there was no need for any defence. That's when I began to see what the problem was. It wasn't so much that Andrew didn't believe in God. From our years of conversation, I had come to know his love of nature, his awe of creation, and his empathy for others. I knew he connected to something bigger. Andrew simply had an issue with the word "God" and the association with the systems of oppression that it has carried for generations. He did not necessarily understand that I had redefined my own understanding of God.

That's when I asked one simple question that changed everything: "Do you not believe that there is some unseen intelligence that connects me and you, connects us to the natural world, and some form of energy or consciousness, beyond labels and systems, that connects all living things?"

He paused, took a moment, and then answered, "Well, of course, without a doubt."

My heart smiled. "Well, my brother, then you are not an atheist."

That evening we agreed that it would be more powerful for individuals to reclaim and redefine their understanding of God rather than deny God's existence. Andrew decided he would no longer allow history to take from him the right to nurture his relationship with the divine, and we noted the importance of encouraging others to do the same.

You don't have to be an academic to see how ideologies of Spirit have historically been butchered, manipulated, and misused. Greed, along with the lust for power, has poisoned our understanding of divine intelligence and unconditional love with fears, separation, and judgements. Organized religion has presented God as exclusive rather than inclusive. I get it. Organized religions have condemned, punished, ridiculed, and even brutally massacred both believers and non-believers in the name of God for so long. In many cases, men of God have become politicians and have turned the love of God into systems of governance. I understand why someone might look at the role of religion throughout history and choose to deny God.

For those who believe in God or adhere to any system of religion, this is not an attack. But if we have any intention of keeping God alive, we must acknowledge the wrongs committed in the name of God and the limiting beliefs that fed them, and do our best to rewrite that programming and heal those wounds. Additionally, if we genuinely desire anyone to come to know God, we cannot allow our identities, labels, or self-righteous egos to get in the way.

On the other hand, it is also important to note the beauty, communion, and magnificence that have blossomed from religions and their various presentations of God. Men and women of God have walked our planet and lit our hearts with unimaginable love. The reality is that it only takes one person's misunderstanding or intentional misuse of power which is never questioned or corrected to create the generational regurgitation that has tainted our understanding of God's love.

While I am not always aligned with the views or approach of organized religion, I do feel God deeply in every cell of my body and every cell of yours. The way I see it, if you acknowledge any intelligence that connects all living beings – an energy of any kind that links us to the natural world or any form of collective consciousness – any concept, form or formless, that may have guided or shaped our existence, I would have a hard time labelling you an atheist.

Divine Possibility

When we declare that we don't believe in God, we shut down any chance of redefining God. You can't redefine something if you say it doesn't exist. In doing so we place limitations on our beliefs and fail to acknowledge any possibility of discovering a more inclusive definition of God. I was once asked if I thought we needed to use the word "God" or if we could refer to our understanding of "divine intelligence" by another name. There are numerous names by which God can be called and has been for centuries. In my opinion, you are even free to make up your own. Ultimately, your relationship with God is unique and doesn't belong to anyone else. However, I firmly believe it is crucial that we also use the word "God". That is the only way to acknowledge the misalignments surrounding our traditional understanding of God and bring light to them. It is always easier to condemn an ideology and walk away from it rather than accept the responsibility to change it. The shift we need in our understanding of

God cannot happen if we turn away and decide to use another name for God. More importantly, we would be widening the separation created by organized religions rather than dissolving it.

Consider this a call to action. It would be sad if we allowed ourselves and future generations to be robbed of the opportunity to connect to something miraculous and divine because we can't separate God from religious dogma. I have witnessed many of my peers refrain from talking to their children about God, or inviting them to converse with God, simply because they, as adults, have failed to redefine their own relationship with God.

> Instead of focusing on how ideas of God have been misrepresented and misused, we can rewrite the story of divinity and nurture a relationship with God that is driven by love rather than fear.

Rather than disassociating from God, we have an opportunity to create a new, inclusive understanding of God that will bring us closer to fulfilling our place in this unimaginable cosmic love bomb. Having conversations that make the space for a new, inclusive, and personal relationship with God opens a whole new world of possibility; a world of understanding, acceptance, and a God that does not divide but unites us. Instead of focusing on how ideas of God have been misrepresented and misused, we can rewrite the story of divinity and nurture a relationship with God that is driven by love rather than fear.

Whenever you encounter the word "God" I encourage you to interpret it as your understanding of God. In doing so, you also give others the space they need to define theirs. Only when we create the space for everyone to discover their unique relationship to God will we begin to recognize our divine connection to each other.

REDEFINING GOD

Chapter 1: Questions for You

◇ Do you pray or talk to God? If yes, what does that look like? If you don't, what do you think has caused you to disassociate from God?

◇ Do you feel that your relationship (or lack of) with God is your own, or was it one that your family and social circles passed down to you?

◇ Can you identify how your perspectives of God might create separation between yourself and those who have different perspectives?

◇ Have you identified the wrongs and injustices that have historically been done in the name of God? Have you questioned them and discussed them? How does it make you feel?

◇ Do you feel comfortable using the word "God", or have you chosen to refer to your understanding of God by another name? If so, why?

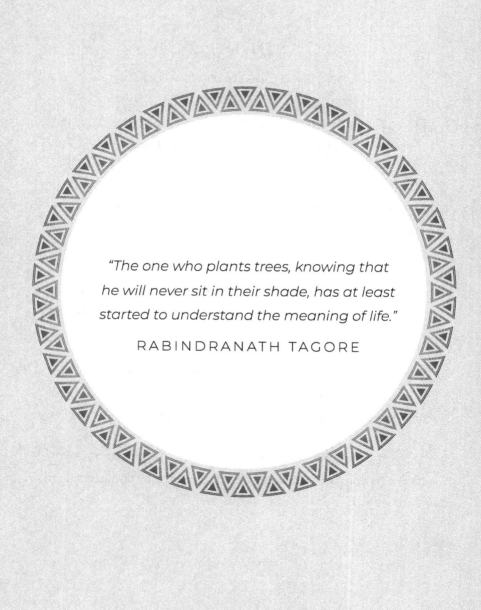

"The one who plants trees, knowing that
he will never sit in their shade, has at least
started to understand the meaning of life."

RABINDRANATH TAGORE

CHAPTER 2

The Illusion of Security

The identity of the individual self is where the desire for security begins and essentially distinguishes you from me and makes us different. It has been called many things and is considered an aspect of the smaller, individual self or ego. In this book, I will also refer to it as the "I-am" narrative. Think of this identity as anything that associates you with your physical body, name, appearance, senses and emotions, place in society, and even the image of yourself that you project to the world. Social factors have conditioned us to believe that we must do everything to attend to the needs and desires of our individual identities, referred to as "I" or "Me". I understand the obsession.

Your physical body and emotions are things you can see and feel every day. From the moment you were born, you have been told it is who you are. Give that a name, and it becomes your identity. "Me Tarzan. You Jane." If it is all you know and identify with, you will naturally serve the preservation and satisfaction of that identity at all costs, because if your identity ever ceased to exist, it would mean that you would cease to exist. With this understanding of your own identity, you take this concept and project it onto everyone and everything else in your life as well. But when we label and identify one another according to these smaller identities and all that revolves around them, we reinforce ideas of separateness and otherness. The concepts of Me and You overshadow the collective We.

As we search for security and a sense of belonging, we create clusters of identities within our communities and among family and friends. The sense of personal identity becomes intertwined with our inner social circles and brings a feeling of We, but it's a We that lives within the confines of belief systems, labels, and commonalities. This We is not a collective one but a limited We that begins to shape the group narratives of Us and Them. For example, one group might create an identity around We-who-are-Republicans, but that We does not include the They-who-identify-as-Democrats.

With these identities forming the foundation of our society, we work towards creating a life of comfort and security for ourselves, our families, and our inner circles. We seek to fill our lives with the things that bring us pleasure, happiness, laughter, acceptance, acknowledgment, and more security. Don't get me wrong, this is marvellous, and we all have a right to create fulfilling and joyful lives for ourselves, but the search for security is ongoing. Everything is secure until it isn't. When it comes to our I-am identities, the only thing we can be certain of is death.

Death often has a really bad rap and can feel heavy, but what if death is not so much an end, but more of a shift or a transition? It is understandable that we experience fear and sadness at the thought of losing the people we love, because we define them by their human identity and form. But the people we love do not cease to exist when death comes. We feel their presence living in our hearts, in our memories, and how they have touched and inspired us. They continue to live within us, through us, and shape who we are long after they have left their bodies. Consider that if we can acknowledge any existence beyond our bodies, then this points towards what our identity is not. Our existence is part of something so vast, intricate, and magnificent that we would not understand even if it was explained in the most elementary fashion. We are not our physical bodies.

Expanding Perspectives

Every human being who embarks upon the journey of introspection will occasionally experience moments when they will be able to say, "God lives here (or there)." It might be a jaw-dropping sunset, a child's infectious laughter, an inspiring conversation, or a selfless act of compassion. But what if I said God lives absolutely everywhere, in everyone and everything? In the light, as well as in what appears as dark. In the sunshine and the minefields of life's pain and struggles. You may be wondering, "How can he say that? How can God possibly live in the suffering, the oppression, the ignorance, abuse, genocide, and inhumane acts of violence?" I'm with you. I get it. I question the same thing every day.

I am not defending or justifying unspeakable acts of violence or the dark aspects of our world. I am, however, implying that the filters of our smaller identities often blind us to a divine intelligence that lives in pain and suffering. The I-am narrative relates to your physical body and everything you experience within your body. It includes anything from your health to your financial security, happiness, opinions, ideologies, and future plans. Naturally, a threat to any aspect of your identity will be considered bad and your reaction will be one of defence. The challenges, struggles, disconnect, pain, and suffering of our lives all fall under the category of "bad" because they appear to threaten some aspect of our identity. Then we apply the same perspective to everyone else's identity and consider anything that threatens their I-am identity as bad.

This narrative, however, is shortsighted and self-centred. I am not saying that these experiences are not painful, but our perspectives are limited to our individual experiences and often to a specific point within our lifetime. What we see and feel is filtered through the lens of one individual, at one point in time, along an infinite timeline. Sometimes we do not consider the centuries of evolution and growth that came before us; transformation born of the hardship, suffering, and even pain of past generations. Furthermore, we often do not acknowledge the potential growth and transformation of future generations that will be born from our present-day struggles. While our current experiences may be unpleasant and painful, they could be someone else's catalyst for growth and transformation.

> Your very own suffering and struggles could be setting the stage and creating possibilities for the transformation of other individuals in your life, absolute strangers, and even future generations.

I am sure you can relate to the possibility of your suffering and hardships playing an essential role in your personal, emotional, or spiritual growth. Just one moment of darkness and struggle may have offered you the necessary tools of transformation to be of service to the world.

What if you were to extend this understanding beyond your I-am identity to your place within a more significant collective identity? If we are part of this magnificent creation and the millions of years of its evolution, aren't our struggles also a part of the world's growth and transformation? Your very own suffering and struggles could be setting the stage and creating possibilities for the transformation of other individuals in your life, absolute strangers, and even future generations.

Kit Kat Kid

If anyone ever asked me to tell a story about India, there would be no question which one: the Kit Kat Kid gave me a heart-opening gift that I am still unwrapping twenty years later. It was my first visit to India, and I had made my way to Calcutta to visit Mother Theresa's tomb and volunteer a little of my time at her orphanage. No, this wasn't some selfless trip to serve those less fortunate. It was on a study-abroad programme called Semester at Sea. We travelled the world on a boat and got a week to explore every country we docked in. This trip to Calcutta was an organized experience and we stayed at a comfortable hotel smack in the middle of Calcutta's world-renowned slums. Our day trips took us to various sites by bus, provided cooked meals, and gave us a glimpse into what poverty looked like beyond a privileged Western filter.

One evening I was returning to our hotel with a few friends after taking a stroll through the markets when I saw him. On the surface, he resembled all the other homeless kids who hung out on the sidewalks of Calcutta: tattered clothes, bare feet, unwashed hair, a layer of dust and dirt on his skin, and begging any passerby in the hope of something to eat or possibly some spare change. But something about this kid was different: he was glowing. Even though his clothes were ripped, filthy, and he probably hadn't eaten a meal or taken a bath in days, he was bright, smiling, and joyful. He ran towards me, and in almost perfect English, with a bob of his head from side to side, he said, "Sir, buy me a Kit Kat. Please buy me a Kit Kat."

When I glanced down to look into his eyes, I noticed he only had one. On the right side of his face, there was simply an empty eye socket that was struggling to heal. While the wound did not appear fresh, it was also evident that it hadn't received the treatment it should have. Trying my best not to seem startled by his appearance and in a little disbelief that he wanted chocolate of all things, I responded, "A Kit Kat?" He nodded his head excitedly and pointed towards a vendor across the road who had an array of unmistakable red Kit Kats displayed at the front of his stall.

After receiving his Kit Kat, the boy indicated that he would escort my friends and me for the next few blocks to our hotel. I was taken off guard by his offer but figured maybe he wanted something else along the way. Little did I know that I was about to witness a simple act of selfless kindness that would be etched in my heart forever. On our walk back to the hotel, that little boy opened his Kit Kat and offered me and all of my friends a bar of it, even before he contemplated having one himself. There were five of us, and a Kit Kat consists of four bars. If we had all accepted the offer to share his chocolate, he would have been left with nothing. As he walked us to our hotel, he continued to offer pieces of his chocolate, guided us away from ditches and holes, and wanted nothing more than our company. When we arrived at our hotel, I turned to thank him, and he smiled with a glimmer in his eye, brought his hands to his chest in a gesture of *pranam*, and bowed.

As it turned out, that Kit Kat Kid wanted to show me that it was possible to love others even when we lack basic necessities and any sense of individual security. Even though he probably wasn't sure where his next meal would come from, where he would rest his head that night, or if he would even make it to see another day, he was willing and ready to share the very little he had.

Collective Security

I am not an astronomer, but I want to bring to your attention that our universe is said to be ninety-four billion light years in diameter, with one light year being nine trillion kilometres. If that doesn't put things into perspective, consider that's only the observable universe. What I'm getting at is that our planet is microscopic, and our individual lives even more so.

While I understand that our individual identity is a significant aspect of the human experience, it is not who we are. We must acknowledge that we are not in this alone. We are all part of a larger collective, like cells in a body, working cohesively to create and maintain a balanced universal system. Each cell is aware of its own little identity, responsibilities, and purpose, but knows that ultimately its duty is to serve the greater whole, something much grander than itself. You and I are cells within that body, and if any cell decided to go rogue and dismiss its role of serving the greater whole for the benefit of its personal agenda, it could disrupt the balance of the system altogether. But if that cell remembers it is part of a bigger network, it understands there will sometimes need to be cell-sacrifice to benefit its greater identity.

In order to elevate the consciousness of humanity, we must consider the well-being of the collective, at times even putting that well-being above our individual needs, desires, and convenience. You may be saying to yourself, "I care about the well-being of everyone." However, the I-am identity is sly and we often consider the well-being of everyone else only after our well-being is safe and secure. Furthermore, we sometimes imagine that our desires and conveniences are necessities and non-negotiables to our well-being, but an honest look might reveal that the surrender of these "necessities" could impact the larger collective in an immensely positive way.

To identify the scenarios in which we might unconsciously choose personal convenience over collective well-being would be unfair, because we all live different lives, with many turning wheels. However, if we are committed to uncovering our unconscious self-centredness, consider: What if everyone did what I did? What if everyone decided to park in the disabled zone for three minutes, drink and drive, skip the line, or buy a new wardrobe unnecessarily? What if everyone placed their own convenience and pleasures above the well-being of others, our society, or the natural world? And felt that they were entitled to do so?

> There is no security in individual identity, there never was, and there never will be. The only security that exists is that of our collective identity.

Of course, there's another possibility to consider – a kinder, gentler one. What if everyone chose to open the door for strangers, made more sustainable choices, and lived less luxurious lives? What if everyone made more effort to feed the hungry, shelter the homeless, or began to consider the impact of their lives and their choices beyond personal desires? What if we all placed social well-being above personal profits?

Throughout this book, we will uncover many aspects of our identity and how they cause unnecessary suffering and inhibit our ability to love one another. When we identify the illusion of individual security, we realize our interconnectedness with all things and discover our true potential to serve. Our hands are held, our hearts are bound, and our minds are woven together by an invisible web of awareness. There is no security in individual identity, there never was, and there never will be. The only security that exists is that of our collective identity.

THE ILLUSION OF SECURITY
Chapter 2: Questions for You

◇ What aspects of your individual identity do you strongly associate with? Imagine completing the statement " I am . . . ." e.g.: I am a yoga teacher. I am Trinidadian. I am a [religion].

◇ How do these aspects of your identity portray you as separate or different from others?

◇ Are there people in your life whom you consider part of your identity or inner circle, and why? How do you treat them differently or maybe give them more attention or allowances?

◇ Are there times when you place the conveniences and desires of your personal identity above the well-being of others? When? How? Why?

◇ How can you begin to extend and dissolve the boundaries of your identity?

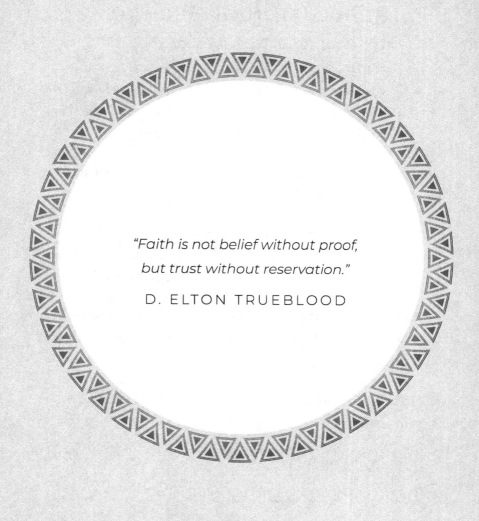

"*Faith is not belief without proof,*
but trust without reservation."

D. ELTON TRUEBLOOD

Faith and Hope: A Tale of Unlikely Friends

The human experience is filled with inspiration, opportunity, and miraculous splendour, but every path is unique, and we are all born into different circumstances that take us through many variations of heartbreak, disappointment, and suffering. Regardless of what our lives look like or how blessed and fortunate our path appears to be, at some point, life will bring us all to our knees, and we will long to overcome the hurt, pain, and despair. The tools of faith and hope are essential to navigating these periods, and while we often consider faith and hope interchangeable, they serve fundamentally different and specific roles in our lives. Understanding their characteristics and function impacts not only our response to life but the resilience and humility with which we navigate it. When it comes to creating the lives we want for ourselves, both individually and collectively, hope would be the wood that awaits the fire of manifestation, while faith would be the flames.

Before we jump into that fire, let's look briefly at the concept of manifestation. Many new-age philosophies have adopted the idea of intentionally manifesting the lives we want for ourselves, and manifestation is often portrayed as a revolutionary realization that can fulfil all our desires. In reality, it's elementary, somewhat obvious, and has been around for millennia. Your actions, words, and even your thoughts shape your experiences, create opportunities, and impact your life in every possible way. You might set your intentions on a new house, a new job, healing a relationship, overcoming heartbreak, dissolving conflict, or bringing more understanding, compassion, and love into the world.

Regardless, we cannot bring our dreams to reality by simply cruising through life, going with the flow, or sitting on the couch with a bag of potato chips. To manifest the lives we want for ourselves and our world, we must bring more awareness to our actions, words, and thoughts to better understand their contribution to our lives. This includes the ways in which we respond to obstacles and challenges as well as our avoidance of them and the growth they offer.

Authentic commitment to manifesting the lives we desire means being present and engaging wholeheartedly with all aspects of our life, both pleasant and unpleasant. In our commitment to do that, it is essential to understand that faith and hope may have the same intention, but do not carry the same weight and often do not result in the same outcome.

Hope

There was a time in my life when I would have been overly enthusiastic to tell you about hope and how essential it was. Hope was always there for me, made me feel better when I was down, and I could always call on her in moments of weakness or despair. Growing up, she always did her best to have my back; but there came a time when hope wasn't enough. While she would always show up and try her best, I would often ask her to fight battles and overcome situations that she simply did not have the means to.

She still doesn't. Hope and I remain great friends, I call on her from time to time, and she will always be there. But I have taken time to understand hope and now appreciate her for all she is rather than what I wanted her to be.

In the past, I had been led to believe that hope could be our salvation in times of despair. That if life brought us to our knees and we kept hope in our hearts, she would pick us up and get us to our feet. But the truth is that she can't; that is not her role. Hope can show us a way out, but she cannot take us there. If we expect hope to create change in our lives and fuel the fire of manifestation, she will burn out, and so will we.

Hope, in many ways, is an essential part of the manifestation process, but only in the very initial stages. When it comes to the fire of manifestation, remember, hope is the firewood. Consider that hope is more of a desire or a longing to manifest something in our lives. She is a dreamer. Hope cannot light that fire and absolutely cannot bring that fire to blaze. It is not her role. She cannot help us overcome challenging and heartbreaking situations, but she does remind us that we can. With our hearts set on our hopes and dreams, there is only one way to bring those hopes to reality. Hope must be accompanied by faith. If we allow ourselves to rely solely on hope to create change in our lives, we

> If we expect hope to create change in our lives and fuel the fire of manifestation, she will burn out, and so will we.

will find ourselves overcome by uncertainty, anxiety, and doubt. Hope does not have the courage and the confidence of faith. When we rely on hope to overcome desperation and struggle without the support of faith, we often end up waiting for something to change without ever initiating that change ourselves.

Kiss of Faith

That afternoon I was devastated. I eased into the parking spot and sat in my truck, getting lost in the roar of the engine and wondering how long the pain would last. I was heartbroken, and her name was Jade.

Earlier that day, I felt defeated. I hadn't been eating, couldn't think straight, and had no desire to pretend that I could function in the world. I couldn't help but wonder what I had done wrong. Was this actually happening? I had given her everything I could for three years and loved her in ways I had never loved anyone before. The questions in my mind would not stop, a constant wondering.

My yoga practice had got me through the last few days, but barely; it was the only thing that could quiet my mind. It took me to a place where I could not pretend, a place where I had no choice but to be vulnerable and feel. That day there was so much to feel, too much. I knew healing meant I first had to fall to my knees and be ripped apart. Avoidance for me was not an option, and with no desire to talk to anyone, I figured I would take my practice to the solace of the ocean so she could wash away whatever needed to come up.

This quiet, magical cove called Macqueripe is no ordinary beach. In a natural display of wizardry, the lush rainforest surrounding the bay reflected on the water, giving it a deep green filter. Massive trees on both sides caressed the long walk down what seemed like an endless staircase. The air was humid, and I could hear the whisper of voices over the crash of waves. Under one arm I had my yoga mat, a towel flung over my shoulder, and a backpack with a wireless speaker and a change of clothes. I knew I had come to the right place, and it almost felt like every step lightened the load I was carrying just a little. I had no doubt a seaside yoga practice and evening ocean dip would lift my spirits momentarily. But I had no clue what was about to go down; I could not have dreamed this up in a million years.

The staircase eased out of the forest canopy and opened onto a serene little hill that gently sloped down to the perfect blend of sandy pebbles. Overlooking the dreamy landscape was a lifeguard hut resembling an elevated shack. It was empty, and the ideal place to practise. Making my way towards it, I waved to a familiar face and tried my best to put on something resembling my usual smile. I wasn't sure what the lady's name was, but I could not forget her perfectly round face, brilliant white teeth against her flawless dark skin, and neatly curated dreadlocks that fell gently to the back of her thighs. She was chatting excitedly with another woman I assumed was a tourist, owing to her pale complexion. European, I would have guessed. Standing between them was a little girl, who turned to face me with stunning blue eyes and an intense gaze that followed my every step. It felt like she saw straight through me into the heaviness of my heart.

Eventually, she cracked a grin as I made my way into the life-guard booth, navigating the two flights of wooden stairs. Standing on the ten-by-ten-foot-square platform, I took a few jumps to test the structure and gave the simple wooden railings a bit of a rattle. It was all good. I set down my yoga mat, connected my wireless speaker, changed my clothes, and it was time, time to get my practice started and time to have my heart cracked open.

I sat on my mat, acknowledged the coming pastel colours swirling in the sky, appreciated the water caressing the shoreline, and closed my eyes. I called on Spirit, set my intentions, and offered my prayer. I moved with focus on every breath, and the moving meditation began. It wasn't long before it seemed like even my thoughts had disappeared into the rolling of waves. I must have been about twenty minutes into my practice when I drifted into a posture called Upward Facing Dog, with my legs energized behind me, pressing into the wooden floor, and my hands rooted under my shoulders. I broadened my chest and slowly lifted my chin – when I suddenly felt I was being watched. I gently opened my eyes to witness the golden glimmer of an epic sunset. And there she was.

As I arched upwards, I found myself looking straight into the bluest eyes I had ever seen. The same little girl I had seen earlier stood no more than two feet in front of me, backed by the wooden railing and a golden sky. While I was somewhat startled, there was a reassuring sense of calm; I mean, she was only three feet tall. I wasn't sure what was happening, and while it was all so strange, I felt like I was looking into the eyes of an ancient sage who could change my life with the touch of a finger.

Unsure how to react, I returned her smile and continued moving into the next posture, Downward Facing Dog. I could hear her footsteps as she began to walk slowly around my yoga mat in circles. She just kept walking around and around as I practised. It was almost as if she had an agenda, knew what she had come to do, and none of this was out of the ordinary. As she continued her walk, I continued my practice, trying my best not to interrupt whatever was happening. After what must have been six or seven circles, she proceeded to sit cross-legged on the floor in front of me. She didn't say a word or display any sign of acknowledging the situation as awkward or strange. She just sat and looked at me practise.

She sat there for almost ten minutes before I eventually came down to my knees, gesturing for her to come over. I asked if she wanted to sit and meditate, but all she did was hold her confident smile, absolutely content to sit and share this space. Her peaceful and non-reactive refusal seemed to communicate, "Please get back to it." Not wanting to make her as uncomfortable as she was making me, I returned to my practice and she continued to look at me as if there was nowhere else in the world she would rather be. It wasn't long before I noticed she had closed her eyes and synched her breath with mine, every inhalation, every exhalation, and pause in between. I felt like I was being transported, and something was moving within me, but I could also feel something moving within that little girl.

I began to hear footsteps coming up the wooden stairs; the floor vibrated with every step. I glanced at her to see her reaction to the person approaching behind me, and then she gestured for them to have a seat beside her. It was the same European woman I had seen with her earlier, and there was no disturbance as she quietly sat on the floor without speaking a word. That afternoon, there was an intimacy that did not need words.

I practised, they sat, and we breathed. I assumed the presence of her mother would have made the little girl feel more comfortable and thought I would again attempt to invite them to join me on my mat. I came down to the floor and took a cross-legged seat, but this time, before I could say a word, the little girl was sliding her way over. She mirrored my position, and then, with a turn of her head, gestured for her mother to join us. We sat there, the three of us, eyelids soft, spine long, and barely breathing. I remember opening one eye to make sure the whole situation was real.

When the silence was broken by the girl's mother it seemed barely any time had passed, but the night sky coming in implied differently. She whispered in French what I imagine indicated that it was time for them to go. We opened our eyes, and I placed my hands to my heart with a smile and offered a gentle bow of gratitude before they began making their way down the wooden steps.

I was still processing the entire exchange, but it was getting late, and I wanted to bring my practice to a close. I found my way into one last Downward Facing Dog, a posture where I take the shape of an inverted "V" with my hips up in the air. Pressing out of my hands and looking under my legs, I could see them making their way down the stairs. When they finally hit solid ground, the little girl stopped and lifted her head to look toward me. She slipped her hand out of her mother's, turned around, and confidently made her way back up into the lifeguard's hut. Before I knew it, there were these two little feet under me as I held my Downward Dog. Tiny toes sprinkled with grains of sand and soft, unweathered skin. She gently placed her hand on my back as if to assure that I did not move, then she slowly leaned over and softly kissed me on the side of my body just below my ribcage. Still, there were no words; angels don't need words.

She turned around and once again made her way down the staircase. It was all so surreal. If I hadn't seen that little girl on my way into the lifeguard hut, I would have thought it was all my imagination, but it wasn't. As I sat there that evening at the end of my practice, something resonated deep within me, a surging upwards of energy and emotion. The sky looked as if God himself had just finished a masterpiece and everything was still. Everything except for the tears streaming from the corners of my eyes.

That was not an experience I could ever forget, but even to this day, I sometimes wonder if it really happened. Fortunately, to be sure I never doubted that experience, I tattooed my ribcage with a symbol of that little girl's kiss in case I ever lost faith again. The despair and desperation I felt that afternoon could never have been dissolved by hope. Hope might have got me through to another day. Hope might have allowed me to dream. Hope would have given me the strength to pretend everything was ok. What I experienced that afternoon was a reminder of what it meant to have faith. A faith that always has your back, a faith that removes all doubt, and a faith that will bring you to your knees from time to time, but will also hold you close and remind you that even your darkest moments are a necessary part of the human experience. This faith has kept Jade and her beautiful family in my life decades later. That angel, at three feet tall, came to deliver a kiss of faith from God himself.

Faith

While often associated with God or religion, it is essential to acknowledge that faith is so much more. Faith does not exist because we choose to believe in God. It's the other way around: faith comes first. It is because of our faith that we believe in anything resembling God. Faith is not merely a desire or a dream, as hope is, it's an intelligence that lives within us, an unexplainable and unshakable knowing. Its reach is far beyond any religious context. Furthermore, the intelligence of faith knows without a doubt that it is part of a more extensive universal intelligence that will assist in manifesting a life beyond our hopes and dreams. This knowing gives faith the commitment and fearless confidence that leaves no room for doubt, anxiety, or worry.

Faith, however, only responds when we wholeheartedly engage with life. She won't fight for you, but she will fight alongside you. When faith has your back, she will lift you up and give you the strength you never knew you had, but first, you must show faith that you are all in. Words are powerful, but they are not enough; you cannot sit on the couch mumbling about your hopes and dreams and wait for them to become a reality. It is the combination

> Faith is not merely a desire or a dream, as hope is, it's an intelligence that lives within us, an unexplainable and unshakable knowing.

and intention of our actions, thoughts, and words that signal to faith whether we are committed or if there is still doubt in our hearts.

As long as we allow doubt to take up residence within us, we will continue to live within the realms of hope. Faith requires absolute and unconditional trust even when facing an uncertain outcome. While we cannot predict the future, that doesn't mean we can't have faith. True faith is bigger than any desire or any specific outcome. Faith insists that we not only commit to manifesting our hopes and dreams, but that we understand we are part of something more significant than our wants and desires.

There will be times when we commit wholeheartedly with faith at our side and still find that our hopes and dreams are denied. These are the moments when we must remember there is a more extensive intelligence or universal consciousness that knows and dreams bigger than we do. These are the times when we discover the power of conscious surrender.

Whereas surrender is commonly considered a moment of defeat or weakness, conscious surrender is quite the opposite. It is that moment when we face defeat, but rather than allowing ourselves to drown in despair, we choose to dwell in humility. That humility acknowledges that we are presented with an opportunity to learn, grow, and transmute moments of despair into lessons of transformation. Conscious surrender is an absolute act of faith and calls us to know without any doubt that she is holding us close and that we are safe, even if our hopes and dreams are shattered, and we find ourselves on our knees. When we face defeat, the conscious surrender of faith guides us to retreat so that we can fight again another day – or maybe realize that there is no need to fight at all.

The reality is that sometimes our dreams are shortsighted, limited, or simply not in the best interest of ourselves or the collective well-being. There may be other things we need to experience or learn, and the truth is that we do not always know what's best. Regardless, as long as there is that longing and desire within us, we must try, no matter how difficult the task appears or how uncertain the outcome is. Faith calls us to engage with life wholeheartedly, and she is not a fan of entitlement. When we put our hands in the air and say, "Oh well, everything happens for a reason," this is very often an act of avoidance and dissociation, not faith. Faith would be taking the time to reflect on what that reason could be, looking for opportunities to grow, and engaging in new possibilities.

With all of this said, it is also essential to acknowledge what I will call "blind faith". There are some things in life we cannot know for sure and others that we have very little influence over. To be over-confident and pretend that we do would be delusional. For example, imagine jumping off a hundred-foot cliff and having the faith that you will land on your feet and walk away. Or having faith that the pizza guy will deliver your favourite pizza, even though you never actually called to place the order. Then there are the times when life holds up a sign that says, "Stop, turn around, do not go this way." But we are so blinded by our faith that we walk straight past that sign, waiting to be guided. These are situations when our faith is blind. In other words, it is not faith at all, but hope that disguises itself as faith.

True faith calls for us to be present, alert, grounded, and aware of the world around us, then to align our actions, thoughts, and words with the lives we hope to create. When it comes to the fire of manifestation, faith is not only the flame but the fuel, a fuel that is driven by commitment, intentional action, and conscious surrender.

The Journey of Shattered Hopes

Faith and hope are essential in manifesting the lives we dream of. Knowing when to draw on the power of faith and how to use it will alter your experience of life and any hardships it might throw your way. When we are guided by faith, we are versatile, resilient, and confident in the face of hardships and struggles. If we live our lives guided by hope alone in the absence of faith, these very same hardships will leave us feeling overwhelmed and defeated.

It was in the jungles of Costa Rica that defeat almost got the best of me when faith grabbed me by the hand, pulled me to my feet, and saved my ass. My ex-girlfriend had planted seeds that inspired me to go on an outdoor wilderness expedition known as Outward Bound. Looking back on it now, I joke to myself and wonder if it was some kind of set-up.

Having recently graduated from university and travelled the world on a ship, I still had a longing for adventure, and, after some debate, I enrolled in a thirty-day Outward Bound trek across Central America. I would begin on the Caribbean coast of Costa Rica, in the town of Limón, and we would walk across the country to heights of more than nine thousand feet before arriving on the Pacific Coast.

Outward Bound didn't exactly tell me what I was getting myself into; if they had given me the details, I probably would not have gone. I knew I would be challenged, and something within me was hungry for growth and transformation, but I was about to discover that this was not a place for hope, and would have to muster the depths and fire of faith to make it through.

We each carried an eighty-pound backpack that contained everything we would need collectively to set up camp, cook food, attend to medical emergencies, and make it to the other side. We walked an average of eight to twelve hours a day, most of the time in the pouring rain. I had two pairs of shorts, two pairs of socks, and two tee-shirts, none of which I ever recall being dry after day one. We washed and cleaned our clothes daily, but the rain never seemed to stop, and the humidity made you feel like a walking fish. The first two days were bearable, but as time went on, the forest grew dense, the rains got more intense, the walks got longer, and what was once excitement quickly turned into disbelief. What was I thinking? Why would I pay for this experience? Tears would often trickle down my face as I walked, daring to imagine what the next twenty-eight days of this reality could hold. I urinated on myself several times, sometimes out of exhaustion and other times simply as a form of rebellion. I ate so much canned tuna that the mere smell of it to this day makes me gag. We weren't allowed cell phones and had no means of communication. At the beginning of our "excursion", we had to surrender all electronic devices, books, or anything that might distract us from the emotions that would come up. We had to feel these emotions, meet them face to face, process them, and pray that we could overcome them before losing our minds.

After about ten days, I was ready to call it quits. It felt like I had signed up for emotional torture and was simply dragging myself through every moment. I felt that completing the trek was no longer an option I was willing to consider, and used every method of internal justification to convince myself that there was no shame in giving up. I began to wonder how I could call home, and knew that if I could just tell my mother of the anguish I was experiencing, her nurturing heart would validate my desire to bail and tell me to get out of there. Even though I had made up every possible excuse in my head to justify my departure, I needed validation, so that it didn't feel like I was giving up without good cause. The reality was that I also needed a plan because I couldn't precisely hail a cab.

It dawned on me that I might be in the middle of the Costa Rican rainforest with no communication or transport, but I had paid to be there. I figured there must be a way to get out, and our two guides must have a way of communicating with the outside world and getting someone out in the case of an emergency. After all, Outward Bound was a well-run and established organization.

It so happened that a member of our group had to be evacuated because his foot got infected, and putting on his shoes became impossible, far less walking across Central America. We were still twenty days away from the Pacific, and our guides presented an evacuation plan to carry him to a nearby village and use a payphone to arrange transport that would take him to a hospital.

It was as if my hopes and dreams were coming true. I couldn't believe my ears, and quickly sprang into action. I explained to the guides that my grandmother was severely ill, possibly dying, and that I had to call to make sure she was still alive or even say my goodbyes. That, of course, was not true. She may have been in her eighties, but she was not ill, and I was pretty sure she was drinking gin and playing bridge, or something of the sort. The plan was that once I convinced them to allow me to make the call, I would tell my mom what was happening, she would validate my desire to leave, and I would jump on that ride into town. Within forty-eight hours, I would be home.

I managed to get that phone call and was buzzing with excitement as if I was already walking through the departure gate, but of course, I could not show even the faintest smile, because my grandmother was supposed to be dying. I huddled in that phone booth, drenched and shivering as my hopes grew brighter with every bringgggg . . . bringggg . . . briinggggg . . . bringgggggg . . . and then finally the deep voice of a man answered. It was Raj, the guy who cut our lawn. I was so excited to hear his voice that I'm sure Raj must have been a little confused. I quickly asked to speak to my mom, and Raj calmly said, "She's not here. She'll be back in about three hours." No one else was at home, and I knew Raj could not give me the validation my heart needed. I didn't even ask about my grandmother, because I knew she was okay. My hopes had just been crushed, and I was shattered.

I had told myself the comforting narrative that if I was unable to get onto my mother, it would be a sign that I had to complete the trek. Now that the reality was setting in, it was a test of faith in every way. This moment was a turning point, and if it had been left to hope, I would have thrown a tantrum and demanded to be evacuated with my co-trekker, or even accepted my fate, dragging myself through the experience miserably, longing for it to be over. Had that been the case, I would have missed the growth and transformation I was seeking. I would never have discovered the greatness that lived within me, and would have lived with a constant regret hanging over my head.

Fortunately, faith stepped in, reminded me that I could indeed do very hard things, and allowed me to see the experience as one that held life-altering potential. It would be my response in that moment which would shape and define the man who would return home to Trinidad. Faith woke me up to actively engage with the experience, knowing that there was a larger vision that trumped my emotions at any moment. Hope, on the other hand, would have allowed me to be overcome by my emotions and led me to dissociate from the discomfort and become numb to any growth it could offer. I still cried and continued to pee myself, while my hair became matted dreadlocks, and I experienced emotions that threatened to tear me apart. But my faith kept me open and gave me the courage to navigate and overcome it all.

The day I felt the sand of the Pacific shores between my toes, the tears came rushing uncontrollably in celebration, joy, and triumph, but there were also tears of shame. I was ashamed that I ever doubted myself, my abilities, my will, and questioned the experience. Those thirty days changed my life, and faith reminded me who she was and what I could do with her at my side. To this day, no matter how high my heart asks me to jump, with faith holding my hand, I'll at least give it a try.

We Are All In

You are in an intimate and ongoing relationship with an undefinable intelligence that is also in a relationship with everyone around you. Regardless of what you choose to call this divine intelligence, as with any intimate relationship, your partner needs to feel that you believe in them. The universe wants to know you believe. If she feels you are fully committed to consciously shaping your life, then she too commits to help you make it happen. Faith is essential if we intend to consciously shape and influence our lives. If we rely only on hope, we are not wholeheartedly in relationship to life but leaving it all to chance. To live with faith in our hearts means that we are fully committed regardless of the outcome. It means there is no need for a fallback plan, a safe zone, or the comfort of security. We are all in!

> Faith is the conscious surrender that turns your despair into lessons of divine transformation.

Even when you are on your knees in desperation, and it appears that you are surrounded by darkness, faith knows better. Faith has the power to dissolve fear, anxiety, and despair; it manifests possibilities beyond hope's limited imagination. Faith is the wind that lifts your chin and restores your heart when your hopes and dreams are shattered. Faith is the conscious surrender that turns your despair into lessons of divine transformation.

One of the greatest spiritual masters, Jesus, once said that if our faith were as small as a mustard seed, we could move mountains. That is not something hope could ever dream of doing. It's convenient and far easier for us to believe this was a metaphor, because acknowledging this teaching as literal truth means that we have a great responsibility on our hands. It calls us to create the world we want to live in rather than allowing life to happen to us, accepting things as they are or hoping that things change. This faith does not discredit your hopes and dreams, but gives you the confidence to manifest dreams far greater than you could ever have hoped for.

FAITH AND HOPE

Chapter 3: Questions for You

◇ With this understanding of hope and faith, do you feel you live most of your life guided by hope or faith?

◇ Where in your life have you been intending to manifest an outcome but not doing anything to make that happen?

◇ In what areas of your life could you possibly engage more intentionally rather than simply allowing things to unfold?

◇ Are there any areas of your life where you may be trying to force hopes and dreams rather than having the faith to surrender to new possibilities?

◇ How did you view hope and faith before reading this chapter, and how has that changed? How do you intend to apply that to your life?

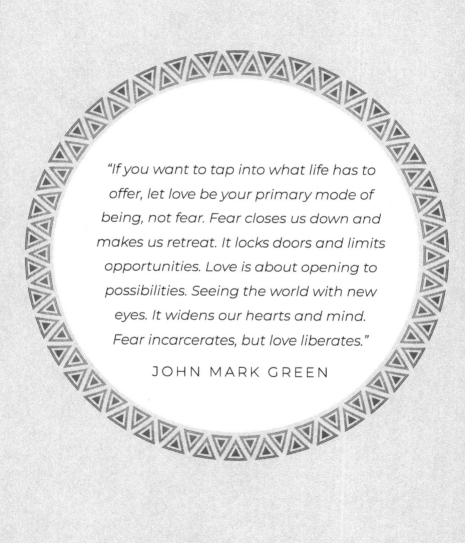

"If you want to tap into what life has to offer, let love be your primary mode of being, not fear. Fear closes us down and makes us retreat. It locks doors and limits opportunities. Love is about opening to possibilities. Seeing the world with new eyes. It widens our hearts and mind. Fear incarcerates, but love liberates."

JOHN MARK GREEN

CHAPTER 4

Love and Fear: The Threads of Our World

First things first: let's wrap our heads around the concept of vibration. Vibrations are at the very centre of our existence. Sound is a vibration. An action is a vibration. Physical matter is vibration. Emotions and thoughts are vibrations.

Both spirituality and science, at their core, agree that our existence began with a vibration. It could be the word of God or the Big Bang, but either way, it was a vibration. The word "vibration" can carry an undertone of new-age mumbo-jumbo, but it's science. All things are made up of molecules and energy that vibrate to create the world we experience. Scientific studies surrounding the resonance theory of consciousness indicate that the vibration of our thoughts, emotions, and feelings can influence the molecular structure of plants, food, water, and other physical matter. Vibrations are real. Even my eighty-year-old mother has come to use the word "vibes" to describe the energy or feeling she picks up from someone. Consider that every decision we make, every thought, word, and action, originates from, and carries with it, a vibration.

Once we can acknowledge that vibrations are everywhere and create our experiences on micro- and macro-levels, the next step is to recognize that vibrations are energy. In the law of the conservation of mass-energy Einstein concluded that: "Energy cannot be created nor destroyed, but only changes state." These vibrations and the energy they carry do not just disappear or dissolve; they will continue to impact and influence our reality until we have the presence of mind to consciously shift them.

A Journey through Silence

From the day you are born, fear begins to lurk in your consciousness. It is a natural and functional part of our programming, designed to keep us out of harm's way. Some fears come to us from birth, as instincts that sound an alarm any time we sense danger. Then other fears might be learned from personal experiences, like the fear of eating contaminated food, getting in a car accident, or falling off a bike.

Fear is essential to our survival and has its place, but if we do not have a wholesome relationship with fear, it becomes toxic. When this happens, we become anxious, unsettled, and pessimistic, while our life becomes routine, heavy, and stagnant; eventually, we are overcome by our fears, and the love of living begins to fade.

When we can cultivate a healthy relationship with fear, it does not mean that our fears disappear. It simply means that we take the time to understand where they come from and precisely what it is we are afraid of. Then we can decide whether those fears benefit us or if they are imagined narratives that create unnecessary anxiety in our lives and limit possibility.

I first felt how tangible this concept was when I decided to partic- ipate in a Vipassana retreat, which is pretty much ten days of silence. All you do is meditate, eat, and sleep. At the time, I had already established a daily yoga practice, but had not yet explored the depth of seated meditation. I figured, what better way than to jump in at the deep end?

I almost drowned.

Never would I have thought that sitting on my meditation cush- ion would bring me face to face with fear. This was not the usual heart-stopping jolt, the cloud of insecurity, or the superhuman rush of adrenaline. This time fear moved in, unpacked its bags, took up residence in my body, and had no intention of leaving. I was sitting on the floor of an old church converted into a Buddhist centre when it seized the opportunity. Right there I became its puppet and it quietly manipulated every thought and emotion.

The first five days of that retreat were absolute torture, and all I could think about was how much longer I had to sit there wasting my life away. My thoughts were tormenting me and constantly writing stories about everything that could be going wrong at home. They were incessant, loud, and seemed to be on permanent rotation. I had created a bubble of negativity and fear around my little cushion, and it became the very last place I wanted to be. The voices in my head sounded something like, "My girlfriend is cheating on me. My friends are surfing and living their best lives while I sit here and waste my life away. My business is going to shit. My grandmother might die (for the second imaginary time). My legs are numb; I won't be able to walk again. What if I die here and never get to tell anyone goodbye? What in the world am I doing?" All that, and yet all the while I sat there in silence, on a cushion, doing absolutely nothing.

While I didn't realize it at the time, almost every thought that bombarded me over those first five days was driven solely by fear.

It took various forms and did everything to get my attention: from body aches, tightness, and anxiety to bathroom runs, hunger, and a whirlwind of emotion.

I could feel the negativity and the resistance building, and while it began as an emotional battle, it wasn't long before this began to have a physical impact. My body became stiff, my energy heavy, I sometimes felt nauseous, and my once-brilliant smile was nonexistent. Spiritually, I felt disconnected, and any light and joy I once carried within me faded. I even began to imagine my escape, much as I had done in the jungles of Costa Rica. I wasn't sure what reason I would make up to justify my early departure this time, but unlike my experience in Costa Rica some years earlier, nothing was keeping me from leaving other than my own will. I could easily have got up, packed my bag, called a cab, and headed for the airport. Believe me, there were many times when I came close to leaving; but something in my heart urged me to stay – something beyond my inability to move my numb legs.

I had read accounts of the transformations others had experienced and heard many individuals speak of the power that came from committing to this Vipassana practice. Fortunately, I did stay, and I did experience a shift. I understand that it's different for everyone, and for me, it wasn't a gradual realization. It exploded like a bomb, followed by one illumination after another. I can't say precisely how it happened, but the realization was initiated by something our meditation guide said regarding fear.

Until that point, I wasn't sure what I was feeling or where it was coming from, I just knew it didn't feel right, and I didn't want it. Our guide had given it a name, and that helped me identify everything I was feeling and thinking: it was fear. I realized that all the negativity I was experiencing came from some aspect of my fears and projection. Up until that point, instead of acknowledging my fears, I was trying to push them aside and shut them up. With this new budding relationship to fear I began to see all the stories I was creating, and could try to understand where these fears were coming from instead of allowing them to overcome me. One thing I knew for sure was that I did not want to live my life enveloped by fear.

However, I had to first identify my fears before I could nurture a conscious relationship with them and have the chance to understand where they came from. How can you have an understanding of – or relationship to – something if you aren't present enough to acknowledge it exists? Only after realizing that I was allowing my fears to shape my reality could I consciously choose love. Rather than focusing on all that I imagined going wrong, I became present to all that was right. If I did stray from the present, I guided my thoughts to create a positive and inspiring narrative rather than one which created suffering and discomfort.

> The only way we can truly commit to love is by having the courage to face, understand, and embrace our fears.

It was almost as if I had looked fear in the eye and embraced it. Fear simply wanted to be heard and comforted, and as long as it was, it would lower its guard and allow me the space to present an alternative reality. The more I deepened my relationship with my fears, the stiffness and aches in my body dissolved, my mind was at ease, my shoulders relaxed, the corners of my mouth lifted, and the rest of my days sitting on that cushion were as harmonious as they could be.

Fear is a negative vibration. While I have felt fear before, I avoided it and never took the time to listen or understand where it was coming from or why. I wanted nothing to do with fear and became so committed to love that I failed to recognize where fear lived within me. That journey through silence gifted me with so much more than a meditation practice. I discovered that the only way we can truly commit to love is by having the courage to face, understand, and embrace our fears.

Identifying Love and Fear

While we often think of love and fear as emotions, I invite you to consider them as states of being. They are the vibrations underlying every emotion, thought, action, and decision. In other words, everything you do, say, or think originates from a place of either love or fear. These vibrations carry with them a frequency we can feel physically and emotionally. They are tangible, and they shift energy not only within us but in the world around us.

Fear carries a negative vibration and a lower frequency, while love has a positive vibration and a higher frequency. You may be somewhat familiar with love and fear, but how they influence your emotions and decisions is incredibly subtle, and recognizing where and how these vibrations show up in your life requires some reflection.

Identifying fear can be difficult because it's common for us to disguise our fears with logic, social norms, and our need for security. Believe it or not, we even find the most creative ways to disguise fear as love. Consider, for example, the fear of change. Our fear of change often shows up as worry and anxiety about what is to come, but sometimes we disguise this fear as love for other things in our life. To put this into context, imagine that your current circumstances are acceptable and somewhat comfortable, but there is so much you would like to change about your life. That change, however, means you have to take risks and even challenge the opinions of your friends and family. You fear not only the uncertainty of what those changes might bring, but also the reaction of your loved ones.

Sound familiar? Imagine that you choose to settle for your current circumstances as they are, because they are safe and you love your family so much that you would rather not risk upsetting them. That choice, however, may not actually be driven by the love you have for your family or your circumstances, but fear of the unknown and your family's reaction.

We will expand on these concepts later, but the fear of the unknown as well as fears surrounding our social acceptance are both fears that often disguise themselves as love.

Beneath the surface, the distinction between love and fear is not black and white. By shifting our perspective, we might discover that the very same actions and words that are driven by fear can also come from a place of love. Furthermore, if we ask ourselves the right questions, we might realize that what we thought was love could actually be fear in disguise.

When I speak about the vibrations of fear and love, I am referring to the intentions and emotions that drive our actions, not necessarily the act itself. While we are not always conscious of the impact that love and fear have on our lives, the only way to realize how they influence us is to identify where they show up.

The Love of a Moon Goddess

I could say that fear and love visit me regularly, but they never leave, to be honest. They are more like roommates that reside in my head, constantly whispering, questioning, and challenging any possible moment of clarity. Love and fear are also some of my most outstanding teachers, and while they generally prefer the subtle approach, they tend to make a scene when presented with the right opportunity.

It so happened that one of these opportunities presented itself on the wings of an extraordinary woman called Kiana – Hawaiian for moon goddess.

It was a casual and organic meeting, and I didn't think much of it at first. Naturally, as a bachelor in my mid-thirties and somewhat ready to settle down, I did take note of Kiana's exotic natural beauty, her elegance, her smile, and the way she gracefully floated across the parking lot. Our initial conversation was brief, but it left me intrigued and curious. As it turned out, the feeling was mutual.

We chatted a little via text messages over the next few weeks, and as I got to know Kiana, my curiosity became admiration. I also discovered that Kiana was a bit younger than I imagined, and I felt a little apprehensive regarding our seventeen-year age difference. However, the more I resisted the feelings I was developing for Kiana, the more fear and love stepped up their game, creating something like an epic Wimbledon tennis final inside my head.

I eventually managed to move beyond my reservations and asked Kiana out. It was a large social gathering, nothing too personal. That social event led to one friendly visit after another. It became clear to us that there was something else developing other than friendship, and neither of us was interested in casual intimacy: it would either be a romantic relationship, or we would just be friends. We had chosen to be cautious and not rush into anything. We considered the goal of a relationship: not necessarily to be happily married, have kids, and stay together for the rest of our lives, but to be about sharing our lives, growing together, filling our lives with joy and laughter, and loving one another beyond expectations and labels. If one led to the other, then we would consider ourselves fortunate.

I did not take the situation lightly. As an established yoga instructor and community leader, I prided myself on integrity and felt there could be a lot at stake for both Kiana and myself. I could not stop wondering what people would say, how they would react, and what they would think. I acknowledged we were at different places in our lives. But underneath all of this was my fear of how it would be received by everyone else and how that would impact us both. I wondered whether it would be acceptable in the eyes of my friends, my community, and my family; then there were her friends and her family. We contemplated what we might be giving up to make it work and considered all the epic possibilities that could fill our lives. It became apparent to us both that all the reasoning about why we should not embark on a romantic journey was driven in some way by fear.

Still somewhat hesitant and seeking reassurance, I consulted a friend – her name was Sara, and I figured if I was missing anything she would set me straight and squash the idea altogether. As a woman who knew what it was like to be in Kiana's position and also knew the ins and outs of my life, I expected her to be totally against the idea. However, after hearing how I felt about Kiana, Sara flipped the situation on its head. She pointed out that if I allowed myself to be overcome by fear and did not follow my heart, I would be going against everything I had been teaching and standing for my entire adult life.

Thankfully, Kiana and I did enter a relationship, filled with many beautiful and unforgettable memories, growth, transformation, and love. Our romantic relationship may have only lasted a year, but the truth is that the intimacy of our friendship will last a lifetime. Looking at the vibrations that fuelled our emotions both in the beginning and at the dissolution of that relationship, we discovered that we chose to be guided by love, but saw how those very same decisions could have also been driven by fear.

When first contemplating whether to enter a romantic relationship with Kiana, I chose to entertain the possibility of love and what I felt in my heart rather than the fears that filled my head. However, that very same decision could have been fuelled by the fear of loneliness or the risk of losing Kiana's friendship.

Towards the end, we again chose love; but this time in dissolving our romantic relationship. We loved each other dearly, and our fears did not want anything to change. Our relationship was comfortable, comforting, and beautiful. There was growth, transformation, and understanding. However, the reality of being at two very different stages in our lives, with different needs and desires, presented a situation that limited us both. The truth is that while we were afraid that we would never find something like that again if we let one another go, staying together would have been a decision guided by fear. Even though I have no doubt it would have been beautiful, we would also have been sacrificing essential aspects of our lives and our personal development. It was not fear that guided us to end our romantic relationship, but love. It was a love of acceptance and understanding, a love that was supportive and encouraging, a love that was not bound by conditions, and a love that was willing to set one another free, even if it meant losing each other in the process.

> What's most ironic about fear is that its gravest worry is not being able to love or be loved.

Fortunately, we didn't have to lose one another, but as the dynamics of our relationship shifted from romantic intimacy to friendship, on many occasions I have had to confront and question whether I was being led by fear or love. You see, love and fear have a special camaraderie with the things and people we cherish, because we fear that we will lose them or have to give them up. They become part of our identity, and fear arises because we feel threatened when our relationship with the things we love begins to change. What's most ironic about fear is that its gravest worry is not being able to love or be loved. So much so, it makes me question if we can truly love someone unless we overcome the fear of losing them.

I trust that regardless of what the future holds for Kiana and me, we will continue to be guided by love as we navigate our individual lives. Fortunately that Moon Goddess is still in my life today, and the reality is that this book would probably never have happened without her continuous support and encouragement.

This story is an example of the various ways love and fear can show up in our lives and how a single action or choice can be guided by fear or love. The only way to identify and differentiate between fear and love is through intimate and authentic introspection. The journey to discovering what it means to love requires us to feel and acknowledge our fears rather than neglect them or push them aside. Then in choosing love, to consider that love does not ask how, when, or why; love just simply loves.

It's Time to Choose

There are countless choices and decisions to be made throughout our lives. A significant source of our anxiety often revolves around what choice is "right" and what choice is "wrong". What will people think? How will everyone react? Will it work out? The truth is we can never know what the outcome of any decision will be, and we can never be sure what would have happened if we chose A instead of B. Sometimes, even after making a decision and choosing A, we wonder what would have happened if we had chosen B. These choices always seem to be a gamble, but they don't have to be.

Yes, fear is sneaky and disguises itself in ways that leave us believing that living from a place of fear is logical and normal. A "normal" we accept so readily, many of us don't recognize our fears without deep introspection and radical honesty, but if we create the space in our lives to be intimate and authentic with our feelings, we can identify the fear. It means acknowledging the situations in our lives causing us anxiety or discomfort, then trying to understand the fear beneath them. Asking ourselves, "What is the problem here? What am I trying to avoid? What am I afraid of exactly? Why would that be so terrible?" Every time we allow fear to guide us, we project a negative vibration into the world and it begins to shift energy within us and around us. When we choose the negative vibration of fear over the higher frequency of love, we become stuck, stagnant, and uninspired.

The good news is that fear only has power over us when it is in the dark. The moment we identify where fear lives, it steps out into the light as if it were playing hide-and-seek. In this game of hide-and-seek, fear wants to be found, it wants to be seen and understood. In understanding and opening the closet of our fears, we reveal another door, the door to love. The more we choose love over fear, the more we project and emit a higher frequency that positively influences our lives. Our lives will align and we find ourselves inspired, calm, confident, and filled with the joy of living. When this shift happens it impacts everything around us and the frequency of love begins to elevate the world's vibration. It is not easy and takes courage, but it is not a gamble in any way. I cannot tell you which choice is the right choice and which is the wrong choice, but if there ever were a wrong choice, it would be the one that is born out of fear.

LOVE AND FEAR
Chapter 4: Questions for You

◇ What are some of the situations in your life that are currently creating anxiety or dis-ease? Why? What are you afraid of exactly?

◇ In general, what are your biggest fears and how do these fears impact your choices?

◇ Where and when in your life do you find it difficult to choose love over fear? Why?

◇ Can you identify a situation in your life where the very same decision could have been guided by either love or fear? Which one guided you in that moment?

◇ In this chapter I suggest that the "wrong choice" is a choice that is governed by fear. In your opinion and in your words, how would you define a wrong choice?

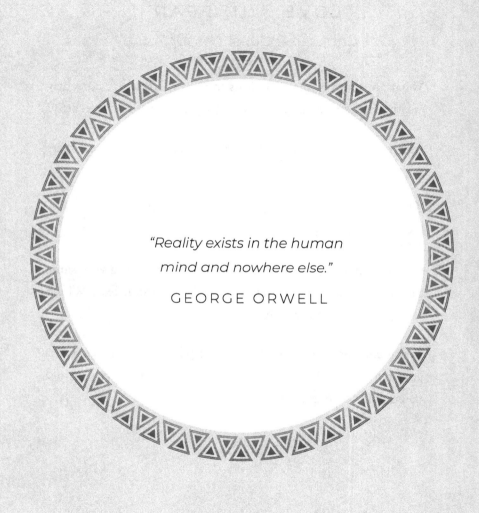

"Reality exists in the human mind and nowhere else."

GEORGE ORWELL

CHAPTER 5

Mind is King

Your mind, without any doubt, is the most underrated piece of machinery on the planet. Everything we know to be true is either something we were told and taught, or information we gathered from personal experience. With that said, we must note that because something may be true to us at any point in time does not actually mean that it is true, or that it ever was. It simply means that we chose to believe it was true, which is enough to make it our reality.

If I chose to believe the colour red was called green, that planet Earth was the eyeball of a fish, or that fairies flew into my mouth and brushed my teeth every morning, then these things would become my reality. They would be true to me. No matter what logic or evidence is presented about any situation, the mind chooses to believe that evidence or dismiss it as false.

However, if left to create your reality on its own without any guidance or supervision, the mind can also be self-centred, emotionally reactive, and delusional. On the other hand, nurturing a conscious relationship with your mind can expand the boundaries of your imagination and become your superpower. Your mind can transform what was once perceived as mundane into absolute magic, and, in many ways, holds the key to your freedom.

This conscious relationship with your mind is like any other relationship, and it can only be nurtured through quality time and intimacy. Quality time with your mind is equivalent to studying the manual of the world's most powerful and influential machine, but we often don't even attempt to open it. Whether you feel that you are at peace with your mind most of the time or possibly find yourself stuck in a reality of anxiety and struggle, either way, there's no escaping your mind, so it only makes sense that you befriend it.

Your Ride or Die

Your mind is your partner for life, kind of like an eternal marriage. However, unlike our common understanding of marriage, separation and divorce are not options. We can't exactly shop around for a new one. Your mind is your ride or die. Your mind could be your best friend, your support system, and your rock; it should not be that scary monster lurking in the darkness waiting to jump you. Spending quality time getting to know and understand your partner is essential to developing a wholesome and loving relationship. Without trust and intimacy, any relationship is destined for a rocky road of power struggles, neglect, and fear. Your relationship with your mind is no different.

Many of us avoid our minds for so long that they behave like neglected children acting out to get our attention. Our minds are on a rampage, screaming, shouting, and writing narratives that feed our anxiety, depression, and disconnect. They are loud, reckless, and out of control.

After almost twenty years of working with individuals and assisting them in navigating their lives, it has become apparent that many people in our society are afraid of being alone with their minds. While there are a lot of things in our world that I consider worrying, the fact that much of our society is not comfortable spending time with themselves is one of the most concerning. When I refer to spending time with yourself, I am not talking about chilling out with your favourite book, binge-watching Netflix, or scrolling through social media. I am referring to real, intimate time without your cell phone, computer, or any external form of distraction. I am talking about real intimacy, reflection, and inquiry. Consider that your relationship with your mind is at the foundation of your relationship with yourself and everyone else.

> We cannot expect to authentically cultivate a loving and understanding relationship with someone else if we have not nurtured that relationship with ourselves.

If we can't be at peace within ourselves, we can't be at peace with each other. Our world comprises roughly seven billion individuals, and each of those individuals has a series of ongoing relationships. Imagine the foundation of each of those relationships being the relationship we have with ourselves. We cannot expect to authentically cultivate a loving and understanding relationship with someone else if we have not nurtured that relationship with ourselves. There are many layers regarding the disconnect and turbulence of our world, but cultivating peace within ourselves is essential if we ever hope to address them.

On the surface, I do understand our avoidance. The mind is the hidden storage space of our trauma, patterns, pain, and a comforting but limited sense of identity. It is the home of everything we would rather forget, and it is often easier to avoid the dark and damaged areas of our psyche. However, we cannot expect to bring light to the dark or heal the damaged parts of ourselves if we don't acknowledge them. We must have the courage to walk into the darkness and find the light switch so we can illuminate all that needs to be healed.

This work can be intimidating, and it's easier to obsess about the work that needs to be done in the world around us rather than within us. Cultivating an intimate and authentic relationship with your mind requires time, vulnerability, courage, and commitment. It is no easy feat, but what choice do you have? If you are genuinely committed to being a better human being and unlocking the full potential that lives within you, then a wholesome and loving relationship with your mind is essential.

Bruno

I could share many stories of mental slavery, victory, and freedom to put this reflection into context, but I don't feel that any of my personal stories carry the weight of Bruno's. His story is truly an inspiring one and I am fortunate that our paths crossed and that Bruno has allowed me to share a brief snippet of his journey. I could never share it the way he could, but I will do my best.

I arrived in Panama a few days before starting a yoga retreat at a beautiful resort called Sansara, and Dayna was an old friend working at the retreat centre for a few months. When she heard I was coming to lead a retreat, she encouraged me to come early and get in some downtime. There was surf, amazing people, and lots of the good-vibe life.

One morning I was sitting with Dayna on the dark, pebbled beach, looking at the waves before paddling out for a surf, when an old four-by-four Hilux SUV crawled onto the beach. It pulled up about fifty feet from where we were sitting, and in the passenger seat was a salty-blond, shaggy-haired dude. "Yes, it's Bruno!" Dayna exclaimed, "I can't wait for you to meet him. I've been telling him all about you, and he has been looking forward to meeting you. He wants you to teach him yoga."

I love meeting new people, hearing their stories, and peeling back the layers that shaped them – especially individuals who have escaped the grind of capitalism and found themselves living by the beach in secluded Central America. However, the scene about to unfold was not something I imagined I would ever see.

Out of the driver's seat jumped an attractive blonde lady, who ran to the back of the truck, pulled out a wheelchair, and pushed it to the side of the passenger door. Bruno opened his door and climbed out of the truck onto the wheelchair, upper body first, using only his arms and hands. His arms, chest, and upper body were significantly larger than those of your average surfer, his legs somewhat smaller. As he rolled himself down to the water's edge, I noticed his wheelchair was modified for the beachy terrain and had larger tyres than usual. I was unsure what was happening until his friend came trotting behind him with a surfboard and what looked like two bungee cords. Bruno used his hands to climb out of his wheelchair onto the sand, positioned his legs in front of him, and strapped them together. Then, propelling himself towards the breakers at running speed on his hands, with his strapped legs trailing behind him, Bruno launched himself into the crashing waves with absolute commitment. When he reappeared bobbing on the surface six feet behind the shore break his pretty side-kick tossed the surfboard over the crashing waves to him. He pulled himself onto it and began to paddle into the lineup as if everything was as it should be. Over the next hour, I sat and watched Bruno catch eight-foot waves and ride them on his stomach while doing turns and manoeuvres just as any other surfer would. I thought to myself in disbelief, "*This* guy is excited to meet me?"

In getting to know Bruno, I discovered that his story, and the physical and mental challenges he had overcome, were far more mind-blowing than what I witnessed that morning. Bruno is a six-time International Surfing Association Paraplegic champion, but he wasn't born paraplegic. Bruno was born in Zimbabwe, grew up in South Africa, and as a teenager found himself spending most of his time at the beach. His love of the ocean made diving, sailing, and surfing essential aspects of his life, and he eventually found himself backpacking to Sumatra, where he became the captain of a sailboat that ran surf charters. As a surfer myself, I want to emphasize that this would be any surfer's dream come true.

In 1998, at the age of 27, Bruno flew back to South Africa on holiday after the Sumatra surf season – a holiday that didn't exactly go as planned. The morning he was scheduled to return to Sumatra, he fell victim to a car hijacking on his way to the airport, and sustained a spinal injury that left him paralysed from the waist down. When he opened his eyes to find himself lying in a hospital bed, the first thing he heard was the doctor saying, "Son, you'll never walk again."

Bruno began to realize he would be confined to a wheelchair for the rest of his life, and slipped into a pit of depression. It wasn't just his livelihood that had been taken from him overnight, but everything that lit his heart on fire and fed his spirit. Not only was he unable to walk, but Bruno was led to believe that he would no longer be able to dive, sail, surf, or spend his time in the ocean as he used to. Not knowing any better at the time, he chose to believe all of the new limitations placed on his life. In the depths of despair, Bruno began to contemplate suicide.

He made his first attempt during a card game when one of his comrades, tired of Bruno's complaining, invited him to pick up a revolver and end it. Bruno decided to take up the invitation, picked up the revolver, and put it to his head. He would at least give it a try, he thought; he had nothing to lose. There was only one bullet in the gun's cylinder. Fortunately, it wasn't Bruno's time, but his struggles continued.

Sometime afterward, Bruno decided he would attempt suicide by drowning. For him, there was no better way to go than in the ocean. But that didn't exactly go as planned either. In his efforts to submerge himself in the surf, he realized that he couldn't swim down very far and found himself constantly bobbing back up to the surface in frustration. He then jumped onto a board and attempted to paddle beyond the initial breakers towards bigger surf, thinking that would definitely take him under. After he was thrashed around by oncoming waves, one of those waves spun his board toward the beach and sent him speeding down the face of the wave towards the shore. At that moment, with the ocean moving beneath him and the whitewater on his back, something changed for Bruno. Feeling the power of the ocean, he describes it as something inside of him being rebooted. That experience shifted Bruno's perspective and he realized that everyone was wrong. He could do everything he loved doing before his accident – he just had to do it differently.

When Bruno had his accident, he was told that he would never do the things he loved doing ever again. However, what sent him plummeting to the depths of depression was that he believed it was true. His reality became one that burdened him and limited all possibilities. It was only when Bruno felt that sensation and rush of surfing again that he realized he could choose to believe differently, and in doing that, he created a new reality for himself. Since choosing this new reality, Bruno has not only become six-time paraplegic surfing world champion, but has sailed the world on a yacht, survived a tsunami, goes scuba-diving and spear-fishing, and in many ways

"If God were to appear and offer me my legs back in exchange for all that I've learned since losing them, I'd kindly tell him that he can keep my legs."

lives his life in defiance of his wheelchair. After living in Bali he moved to Panama, where he opens up his home to assist in the rehabilitation of others with physical disabilities. His hope is to facilitate their journey to healing by introducing them to some of the ocean medicine that changed his life.

I recall chatting with Bruno one night in Panama about his experience, struggles, and journey. He told me, "If God were to appear and offer me my legs back in exchange for all that I've learned since losing them, I'd kindly tell him that he can keep my legs."

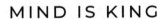

MIND IS KING

Chapter 5: Questions for You

◇ Can you identify some of the things you have chosen to believe simply because you have been told they were true but can't actually prove as fact?

◇ Are you comfortable spending time with yourself and your mind? Do you create space to do so? How? And, if not, why not?

◇ What are some ways your mind manifests a reality that creates unnecessary stress, unpleasant experiences, or feeds disconnect in your relationships? How can you shift those beliefs in a way that could positively influence your life as it did for Bruno?

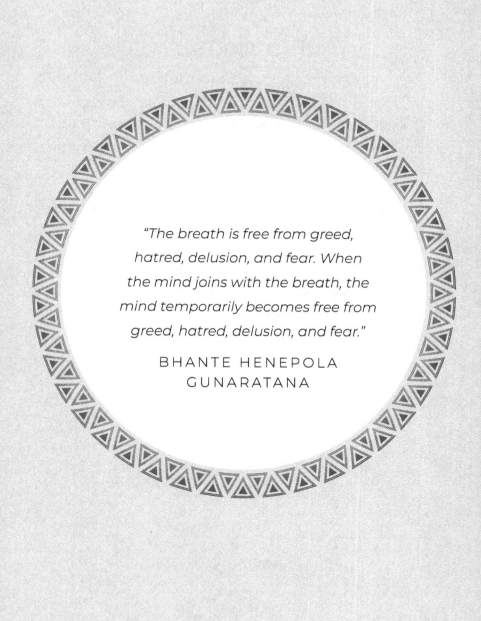

"The breath is free from greed, hatred, delusion, and fear. When the mind joins with the breath, the mind temporarily becomes free from greed, hatred, delusion, and fear."

BHANTE HENEPOLA
GUNARATANA

Being, Not Doing

The Mind Speaks

All this talk about cultivating an intimate relationship with the mind is beautiful, but we must understand what that means. Naturally, because every relationship is unique, spending quality time with our minds might look a little different for each of us. Regardless, it is essential to remember that quality time means one-on-one, you and your mind. It means creating a space where you can listen to, acknowledge, and understand your thoughts, fears, and emotions without judgement of them. There are many modalities and approaches that give us the tools to cultivate this relationship with our minds, but the very core of this relationship calls for vulnerable and authentic listening. In other words, something resembling meditation.

Meditation practices come in various forms. However, to many people, the idea is scary, carries its own stigma, and may even cause you to roll your eyes in dismissal. I'll never forget my brother's fright when he first saw me meditating. I must have been about nine, and something had inspired me to erect an altar in the corner of my room surrounded by candles. My brother, who is ten years older, walked into my room to see me sitting cross-legged in front of this altar with burning candles, and screamed, "Mom, come quick, something is wrong with Troy!" – a sentiment I am sure he sometimes feels up to this very day.

The resistance some of us have towards meditation usually arises from a misunderstanding of what meditation is or the frustration experienced when we realize how hard it is to be with ourselves. Either way, it is often because we have been trying to *do* it rather than *be* it. Meditation is not an act of *doing,* but of *being.* In other words, you can't do it wrong, but it will surely help to understand the essence of what it means to "be in meditation".

When you first embark on the journey of meditation, it's common to feel that your mind won't shut up. You then might feel defeated and overwhelmed by the whole process and find yourself thinking, "I'm wasting my time; nothing's happening. I must not be doing it correctly. This is impossible! My mind just won't stop."

If you were to neglect your partner for years and finally have the courage to sit and meet face-to-face, it's to be expected they would have a lot to say. Even if your name were Buddha, you would get an earful when you eventually sat to be with your mind. Remember that you are cultivating and sometimes even mending a relationship with your mind; it will take time. Regardless of how much your mind has to say, I am assuming that you'd never go home to your spouse or best friend and tell them to shut up. At least, not unless you were trying to pick a fight, or prefer to sleep on the couch. In any relationship, we need to be heard, to know that someone is listening and trying to understand. Your mind wants the same thing from you. That is all that meditation is. The intimacy that comes from genuine and authentic listening in any relationship is profound; your relationship with your mind is no different.

Think of meditation as simply sitting and spending time with your mind, listening to what comes up, observing where your mind goes, and just being present without judgement. Notice what emotions arise and how they make your body feel. The natural state of the mind is to create, and, from time to time, it is normal for our minds to take us on a ride, but the more we attempt to listen and understand, the less the mind needs to scream and shout. The mind becomes more receptive and the relationship becomes one in which we can consciously influence the mind, its perspective, and its response to the world around us. However, to communicate efficiently and clearly, listening alone is only part of the process. We must learn to speak the language of the mind, and that, my friends, is the breath.

World-renowned yoga teacher B.K.S. Iyengar, with his expected clarity and directness, said, "Your mind is king of everything, but breath is the king of your mind." We have acknowledged that your mind creates your reality and therefore in many ways, your mind is king, but your breath is the one thing that can tame your mind. If your breath is conscious, deep, smooth, and easy, then your mind begins to follow suit. If your breath is unconscious, shallow, and fast, your mind is free to indulge in its vices (usually to your detriment). To have any chance of true intimacy with your mind, a conscious relationship with your breath is essential.

Being Breathed

The gift of breath comes to us at birth, and there's nothing we have to do; it's automatic. However, the involuntary act of breathing is very different from being in relationship with your breath and breathing consciously. I was twenty-seven when I learned how to breathe, thanks to an online anatomy course with yoga teacher and author Leslie Kaminoff, founder of The Breathing Project. My intention was simply to expand my knowledge of anatomy to be a better yoga teacher; I never imagined I would learn to breathe for the first time. It turns out that the anatomy of my breath and the power it held were things I was never taught growing up. Not in school, not as an athlete, and not even during yoga-teacher training. But once I began to understand the breath more intimately, it not only impacted my relationship with my mind, but changed my life.

This chapter is about the mind and its power, but since breath is king of the mind, it makes sense to take a quick look at the fundamentals of breath. You may discover that your breath is more of a gift than you had previously realized.

If you were asked to identify the areas of your body that you breathed into, most individuals would probably identify their abdomen or chest. However, few individuals would identify both these areas, along with the side-body, back-body, and everything in between. While the breath descends into the lower abdomen towards the belly and then fills the chest cavity, the full potential of your breath expands horizontally through your ribcage and even moves into the back of your body. Think of your ribcage like the gills of a fish and imagine breath filling your upper body like a cylindrical canister in every dimension possible.

When we inhale, our diaphragm, the umbrella-shaped muscle attached to our ribcage, descends into our abdominal cavity (belly). While some may refer to this as belly-breathing, it is essential to note that we do not breathe into our belly. The only reason our abdominal cavity expands when we breathe is because our diaphragm descends and applies pressure on the abdominal region from the top down. While the diaphragm is considered the most efficient muscle that contributes to respiration, it is not the only muscle of respiration. The full capacity of our breath can only be achieved when the accessory muscles of breathing are used to expand the side, front, and back body in addition to the descent of the diaphragm.

To make more sense of this, let's look at the physics associated with the breath. What if I asked you whether the act of inhaling was a pull or a push of air? Pause for a moment if you like and take a long, smooth inhale. The majority of people would interpret the inhale as the act of pulling air into the body, but that's not as accurate as you would think. While it may feel like you are pulling air into your body, let's understand what is happening beneath the surface.

How the breath works is more like a natural vacuum, and there are two laws of physics that are essential to understand. The first is Boyle's law, which explains that volume and air pressure are inversely related. In other words, as volume increases, pressure decreases, and vice versa. The second is that gases will always move from high pressure to low pressure and this is the law of nature that causes wind.

Now let's put this into context. With the descent of the diaphragm, the expansion of your ribcage, the lift of your chest, and the expansion of your back-body, an increase in the volume of your thoracic cavity (the area that houses your lungs) is created. With this expansion of your thoracic cavity, the air pressure inside your lungs decreases so that it becomes lower than the air pressure in the atmosphere around you. This difference in air pressure causes the air in the atmosphere to move into your lungs, from high to low pressure. Therefore, the act of inhaling is not a pull of air but a push of air. It just so happens that we are not pushing or pulling the air ourselves; we simply create the space to receive that push of air.

The act of breathing is not something we do on our own. We exist in relationship to the world around us, and as long as we create the space within our body to receive breath, it will be gifted to us. We are breathed by something externally, and the more space we can create within our bodies, the more breath we can receive. As if that weren't magical enough, the same force breathing you is the same force that breathes me.

It would be impossible to unlock the mind's full potential without nurturing a conscious relationship with your breath. The breath speaks the language of the mind, and these two are more interconnected than we may ever understand. Together they share an intelligence that will change your life.

Meditation Won't Change Your Life

It may be hard to imagine that just ten to twenty minutes of meditation a day would change your life. That's because it won't. It will, however, change your relationship with your breath and mind, and *that* will change your life. Meditation deepens your relationship with your mind and your breath in a profound way, but that is just the beginning. What use would it be if that relationship did not shape how we showed up in the world every day? Are you going to sit in a cave and meditate for the rest of your life?

As we navigate daily life, our minds and emotions constantly influence our state of being as they react to the circumstances and situations we encounter. However, the nature of this relationship is usually unconscious, automatic, sometimes emotionally reactive, and often fuelled by insecurity, anxiety, and fear. By cultivating an intimate connection with our breath, we nurture a deeper relationship with our mind, allowing us to respond to life consciously, rather than reacting unconsciously. Essentially, we begin to take our meditation practice into our lives so that we are able to live more mindfully and intentionally. Over time our lives become a living meditation.

Short Breathing Practice

Sit up tall and elevate your hips in line with or higher than your knees. You can sit on a chair or elevate your hips with a cushion or blanket.

Without controlling your breath, look at your breath and how it moves through your body (for two minutes).

Begin to engage with the breath slowly. Direct the breath through your nose in a smooth, gentle manner. Use the steps below as a guide.

1. Come to the bottom of your exhalation and pause the breath. In your next inhalation, feel the diaphragm descend into your abdomen.

2. As the breath begins to move into you, feel your ribcage expand like the gills of a fish, feel the expansion of your chest and sternum, even feel the broadening of your back and shoulders.

3. Notice that the taller you sit, the more space you create in your torso, which increases your capacity to receive breath.

4. When you have comfortably created all the space you can and are filled with breath, pause and gently allow your body to contract and release the breath. (Repeat for as long as you like.)

   ◇ Remember that it is not a competition. You are in a relationship with your breath, and the last thing you want to do is build tension or bring aggression to that relationship. Listen to your breath, feel your breath, and imagine that it carries with it an emotion. Imagine that emotion to be supportive, compassionate, and loving.

> An intimate relationship with your breath and mind gives you back your freedom. Without it, life becomes an automated series of routine and reactive experiences.

To live mindfully becomes an ongoing practice, rather than something we do from time to time.

In his book *Man's Search for Meaning*, neurologist and psychiatrist Viktor Frankl said, "Everything can be taken from a man but one thing: the last of human freedoms . . . Between stimulus and response, there is a space. In that space is our power to choose our response. In our response lies our growth and our freedom." An intimate relationship with your breath and mind gives you back your freedom. Without it, life becomes an automated series of routine and reactive experiences.

I believe that, on some level, we know that exploring the depths of our internal universe will reveal a power that is far beyond anything we could have dreamed; a power that forces us to acknowledge our responsibility and to take accountability for the world we are creating. I imagine that is why it is often easier to occupy ourselves with the external world. The peace and harmony we would like to see among all people cannot be found without understanding and befriending our minds. As the great mystic poet Rumi once encouragingly asked, "And you? When will you begin that long journey into yourself?"

BEING, NOT DOING

Chapter 6: Questions for You

◇ Have you ever attempted any form of meditation practice? If yes, how did it make you feel? If not, why?

◇ Has this chapter in any way offered you a new perspective on breath? If so, how?

◇ Do you see benefit in sitting quietly with your mind and breath for even five minutes a day?

◇ When are you going to begin/resume a daily practice of being with your breath and mind?

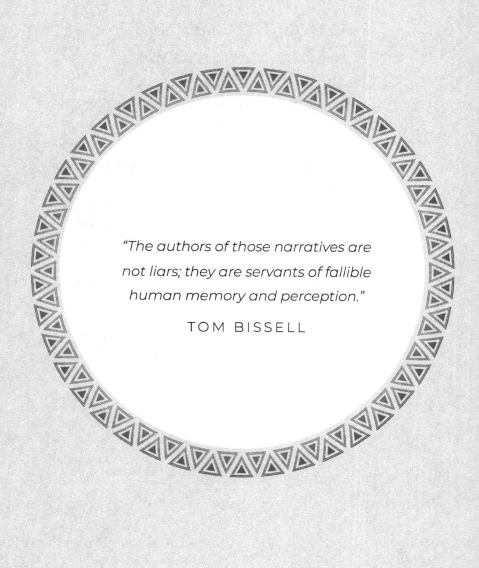

"The authors of those narratives are not liars; they are servants of fallible human memory and perception."

TOM BISSELL

CHAPTER 7

The Narratives
that Blind Us

Think of a narrative as a story about who you are, how the world works, and what you can expect from pretty much anything or anyone. Once we understand the mind's power to shape our perspectives of the world and, by extension, create our reality, we can begin identifying the narratives we have chosen to believe. We all have them. Some of these narratives we've been told from the day we were born, others we pick up from social influences, and some we even fabricate ourselves from experience. While any narrative could once have been true, that doesn't mean it is still true today. It doesn't even mean those narratives ever served us or society. Sometimes narratives have had agendas that benefited an individual, a select group, or have been intentionally crafted to sway public opinion or perspective. With that said, not all narratives are false, deceitful, or ill-intended. Some have the greatest intentions but have simply been crafted through the conditioning of limited and self-centred perspectives.

Regardless, if we buy into all narratives without question, it means that we assume everything we've been told is true. We end up repeating the wrongs and mistakes of past generations and find ourselves accepting the misinformation and misalignments of our society as normal. That, of course, is not only unfortunate but dangerous, and it has been happening for aeons. Unfortunately, it is still happening today. The good news, however, is that these narratives have not blinded us and that we have only been blindfolded. We now have a responsibility to remove that blindfold and rewrite those narratives.

Social Narratives

Social narratives are everywhere. They are embedded in our systems as laws, social norms, expectations, labels – and they have a much greater hold on us than we want to admit. While some of them have their place and do serve our society, many do not benefit our well-being or the greater collective. In many ways we are governed by a system of social norms and narratives, ideas that tell us what our lives are supposed to look like and what boxes we should put ourselves into. These narratives label us as individuals, promise us "freedom" and, ironically, manipulate that freedom by telling us what to do, what to say, and who to be.

Where did we get the idea that we should eat three meals a day rather than just eating when hungry? Who told you that you are supposed to get married and

> We are governed by a system of social norms and narratives, ideas that tell us what our lives are supposed to look like and what boxes we should put ourselves into.

have a family, or that any particular race or religion is more entitled than others to God's love? Do you believe that all politicians are greedy and corrupt, or that all major corporations are unethical by nature? Why do so many of us consider our careers and financial freedom the ultimate measure of success? How about the assumption that the homeless guy on the street is a drug addict, that he knew better and could have made different choices? Where did the idea come from that you should fear God?

While some social narratives have merit, they are not absolutes, and we must question them all. Many of the practices and ideologies that were once accepted and even encouraged are not only illegal in today's world, but are considered inhumane or are simply unimaginable. These ideologies were once considered normal and acceptable, until they were questioned, challenged, and condemned. In his bestseller *Sapiens*, Yuval Noah Harari reminds us that even though a narrative or practice has been taught and retold for thousands of years, that does not make it right or justifiable. Consider the caste system, gender inequality, racial segregation, and religious genocide. While these issues may still exist in our world, imagine if they had never been questioned and were still considered tolerable or customary. You can even try to wrap your head around the fact that cigarette smoking came doctor-recommended for over twenty years.

When it comes to social narratives and norms, we must reconnect to what we feel is in alignment with our beliefs and question who and what that serves. If we believe strongly in any perspective, opinion, or ideology, it is essential that we ask ourselves why. Is it a narrative we have been told? Where did it come from in the first place, and who does it benefit? Then, in your inquiry, be aware that we sometimes have subtle unconscious agendas that don't always consider the collective. While these personal agendas are often unconscious, they influence our views and beliefs.

For instance, imagine a second-generation oil tycoon who has lived his entire life in luxury and comfort fed by the fossil-fuel industry. He has always been told that global warming was a hoax and that renewable energy was not financially sustainable. Conveniently, he chooses to believe this narrative, despite credible research and data to the contrary. If he chose to believe or even consider otherwise, it might threaten not only his livelihood and that of his friends and family, but also his identity. Even though he may not be conscious of his conditioning, the narrative he has come to believe is not based on fact but on his identity, agenda, and convenience.

We can probably imagine countless examples where our narratives disconnect and blind us to what is really happening. The dissolving of social narratives can threaten someone's security and sense of identity, even our own. Challenging them is not easy, and the effort will more than likely, at some point, meet resistance. However, if we discover that any aspect of a social narrative does not serve the greater collective, then we have a responsibility to dissolve it, or at least try to.

The Closet

Social narratives influence us in various ways, and they come with their blend of perspectives, opinions, and filters, according to our upbringing and surroundings. As we grow into adulthood, sometimes we begin to dissolve these narratives through our introspection and observations, but there are other times when someone pulls the blindfold from our eyes.

During my sophomore year at university I had one of my most memorable experiences of having that blindfold gently removed, something I celebrate to this day. In many ways, my views on homosexuality had been shaped by my upbringing. Not only was I brought up in a Catholic home and educated in Catholic schools, but in the

Caribbean, the general manner of thinking is relatively conservative and somewhat closed-minded. In other words, social narratives carry a lot of weight and are immensely influential. I can safely say that in 1998, Trinidad and Tobago was not a welcoming place for anyone to be openly gay. There was ongoing discrimination, name-calling, ridicule, harassment, and violence.

An additional influence of my conditioned narrative on homosexuality was Caribbean reggae and Rastafarian culture at the time. Reggae culture played a significant role in dissolving many of my other social narratives, but many within it viewed homosexuality in a negative and hostile light. Before attending university at seventeen, I can't recall genuinely getting to know anyone who was openly gay, and had no real opportunity to question that narrative. My knowledge of the LGBTQ community and their lifestyles came solely from television and social influences.

Fortunately, from a young age, I understood that discriminating against anyone for any reason was not acceptable, so I always tried to be kind and cordial towards anyone I thought might be gay. However, what I did not realize was that treating one group of people with kindness and tolerance, and another group with love and acceptance, is in fact discrimination. At university, for the first time I had friends who were openly gay, and while I loved and appreciated them dearly, I never made a conscious attempt to understand. I never asked what it was like being gay, how they felt, or why. I think a part of me simply wanted to pretend that they weren't gay, and another part of me thought that my tolerance was love and acceptance.

It all began to change one sophomore night with a heartfelt conversation between two friends. Her name was Amanda, and she was straight, beautiful, and rebellious. We were reasoning about life, God, and all things philosophical, as we often did, when she asked about my views on homosexuality. Being from the Bahamas, she was familiar with the standard Caribbean narrative, and asked if I thought homosexuality was wrong. I recall beating around the bush a little and explaining that I would never treat anyone differently on the basis of sexual preferences, and felt that everyone had the freedom to make their own choices. But then she asked again if I thought it was wrong to be gay. To my disappointment, I said yes. That's when Amanda pulled the blindfold from my eyes. She asked, "But don't you believe in unconditional love?"

I replied with a resounding, "Yes."

Then she asked, "Have you ever been in love?"

Part of me wanted to tell her I was falling in love at that very moment, but instead, I replied, "Absolutely. Of course I've been in love."

Then, in a soft voice, she offered, "Well, did you fall in love with a person or a gender?"

That was all it took. Right there and then, that narrative began to fall away. I remembered that love had no labels or conditions, and that the true essence and spirit of an individual, the soul that we fall in love with, is much larger than our physical identity. I questioned the views I had held for so long regarding homosexuality and started to see all the double standards and narratives surrounding them. Where did that narrative come from in the first place? On a personal level, how did I truly feel? What was I missing?

From that day forward, I sought to understand my friends and individuals who identified as part of the LGBTQ community and discovered some of the most phenomenal people I had ever met. Thankfully, they helped bring some light to my conditioning and how I had been unconsciously contributing to discrimination. That process is ongoing to this day. Even after we identify our narratives and conditioning, overcoming their hold on us does not happen overnight.

Even though the social narratives surrounding the LGBTQ community may be very slowly changing, it is not happening quickly enough. The fact that anyone feels a need to hide in a closet because of their sexual orientation tells not of their brokenness as individuals, but our brokenness as a society; brokenness that every one of us must play a part in healing.

Direct Narratives

"Direct narratives" refers to the stories we write about other individuals, as opposed to groups of people, and boy, are we good at it! It could be a friend, family member, celebrity, or someone we have never met. These direct narratives are just as powerful as our social narratives, and their impact on our relationships can be even more immediate and tangible. The good news is that the root of a direct narrative is close to home because we are the ones creating it. While this can make them easier to identify and address, we are often resistant, because it means taking responsibility for the narratives we have created and realizing how we contribute to stereotypes, wrongful assumptions, and disconnect within our relationships and our society. In no way is that a comforting realization.

We create these narratives about someone else's beliefs, personality, character, and even intentions. While social factors can influence personal narratives, they are also fed by our personal experiences. Here I am using the term "personal experiences" loosely to include the experiences of our social circles, family, and any of our five thousand "friends" on Facebook. In other words, gossip. Someone shares their experiences with us and then we adopt the narrative that comes with them as our own.

Furthermore, consider that every personal experience is interpreted through a series of filters. These filters are shaped by our expectations, influenced by past experiences, and often exaggerated by an emotional lens, according to how they make us feel. Using this information, we create a narrative about someone based on our interpretation, assumptions, and even our unconscious agendas and biases, or those of our peers.

However, in crafting these narratives, there is so much that we often do not consider. We interpret someone's actions through our filters, but don't always take the time to understand someone's intentions. We have no idea what situations they might be currently navigating in their own lives or what they might have to consider regarding the impact of their choices. Imagine that sometimes we attach an entire narrative to an individual based on a two-minute interaction, a story from their ex, their vaccination status, or because they have twenty thousand followers on social media. Maybe we've labelled someone as self-centred, closed-minded and ignorant simply because they didn't agree with our perspective or support our agenda.

Don't get me wrong: learning from our experiences is an essential part of our survival and imparts a level of knowledge that assists in navigating our lives, but we would be greatly mistaken if we assumed that our understanding of any situation or individual based on our past experiences is always true. Whether it comes from personal experience, stories from friends, or your imagination, labelling anyone with a narrative denies them possibility.

> It would serve us to identify and dissolve the narratives we write about individuals we have never taken the time to understand.

This possibility is our birthright and while it includes the right to learn, grow, and do better, that means it also allows us the right to be human, make mistakes, and have a bad day. To take that away from someone not only robs them of their humanness but also, in many ways, robs you of your own.

Understanding someone's intentions and creating this space for possibility calls for us to put our narratives aside and have authentic conversations. This opportunity may not always present itself, but in the meantime, it would serve us to identify and dissolve the narratives we write about individuals we have never taken the time to understand.

Schooled in a Gas Station

I've always believed that some of our greatest teachers appear to us in the most unexpected ways, especially when we are resistant to someone or something. The following story is a testimony to that.

After refuelling, I jumped back into my truck and eased straight ahead into a parking spot outside the gas station's convenience store. While sitting in my truck, having a somewhat frustrating phone conversation, I saw a man approaching my window from the rear of my vehicle. He had a limp and was rather shabby in appearance. From my past experiences at that gas station, I assumed he was coming to ask me for money that would satisfy his habits. I felt that the least the man could do was wait for me to get off the phone and out of my car. I saw the scene as a threat to my personal space.

Even though I saw it happening, I was in disbelief when the man reached my door and began knocking on my window. My instant response was irritation, and I quickly shot him a wide-eyed glance and drew his attention to the phone against my ear. As I turned my head away from the window and returned to my already challenging conversation, I couldn't help but notice that he just continued to stand there. It wasn't long before he knocked on my window again, edging my frustration towards the realm of anger. I waved the man away aggressively, while indicating that I had no cash. In response, he simply took a step backward and looked at me with a gaze that bridged disappointment and fury. What confused me further was that it appeared he had the nerve to mirror my frustration.

The man began to breathe deeply and calmly stood there with his eyes fixed, patiently waiting for me to get off the phone. Fortunately, the rest of my phone call was brief, and it wasn't long before I wound down my window and tried to muster as much compassion as I could before giving the man a piece of my mind.

"My brother, can't you see I was on the phone? Couldn't you have waited until I got out of my truck? I have no cash on me. I can't help you today."

The man smiled softly with what I interpreted as an apologetic dip of his chin. In reality, though, he was simply allowing me the space to discharge my frustration before he pulled my head out of my ass. With a soft and caring tone, he replied, "Sir, I am sorry that I interrupted your phone call, but I pulled up at the pump across from you and noticed that you left the pump nozzle up and the meter running on your credit card when you drove off. The next person who pulls up at that pump will be fuelling their vehicle at your expense."

Overcome with the weight of embarrassment, I took a moment before finding the courage to apologize and express my gratitude. What I probably should have done was hand the man my credit card along with the keys to my truck, because that lesson was worth more than either.

That man was an embodiment of loving-kindness – and I saw a threat. I had been so conditioned by my past experiences that I created a narrative which tainted my experience and blinded me to who he was. I saw a predator where there was a teacher, and I fabricated a confrontation where there was an offering of love.

Self-Narratives

The question "Who are you?" can often ignite excitement and eagerness to tell your story, but what you're telling is precisely that: a story.

More importantly, it's a story that is still unfolding, and you are writing it. Who you are is not the same as what you do, what you like, or even what you believe. All aspects of our smaller identities can change, and while they may define us at any point in time, they do not define who we are or, more importantly, who we can become. If you become attached to the narratives you create about yourself, it can lock you into a box and limit your very own possibilities.

To become the version of ourselves that we dream of, we must first identify and dissolve the limiting narratives we tell ourselves every day. These limiting self-narratives are often shaped by social influences as well as the opinions of our friends and family. These influences have categorized us, told us what career we should pursue, what we are good at, how to dress, what to think and who to love. From a young age, these influences try to tell us *who we are*, and in many ways, we have been allowing them to do so.

As an eight-year-old kid, I was kicked out of the school choir and told I could not sing. All the other kids attended choir twice a week, but I had to find something else to do with my time. That narrative has travelled with me my entire life, even though I come from a family of extraordinary musicians. My older brother happens to be one of my favourite singer-songwriters on the planet, and I have often been asked, "How come you don't sing? How come you don't play music?"

I would always imply that I didn't have the desire to play music, but the truth was I didn't dare to rewrite the narrative. I allowed myself to believe that I couldn't sing or play music. Recently, though, I bought a harmonium and decided it was time to rewrite that story. Thanks to a friend who is an epic musician herself, I am even entertaining the possibility of up-levelling my new story. She told me I would sound like my brother if I were to sing, and I believed her. That day I officially became a vocalist and perform in my car every morning after two double espressos. Voice training is now on my to-do list; the only one who can take it off that list is me.

When considering your narrative, remind yourself that you get to write it. Regardless of your influences and experiences, you can consciously choose how you allow these influences to shape you. You choose which narratives serve *who you are* at any moment and, more importantly, who you would like to become.

> If you have a vision of your life and the person you would like to be one day, the first thing that needs to change is the narrative that tells you why you can't or shouldn't.

Taking an honest look at what you believe about yourself allows you to identify the narratives holding you back from becoming the person you want to be. Some of these narratives may even be secure and comforting. They may allow you to play it safe and believe that you weren't good enough, had other responsibilities, or that the stars don't align. Maybe what's holding you back is a relationship you should have left years ago, but you've told yourself you couldn't do any better. Or possibly it's a job that no longer inspires you, and you have allowed yourself to settle for security. If you have a vision of your life and the person you would like to be one day, the first thing that needs to change is the narrative that tells you why you can't or shouldn't. Then, as you create space in your life to rewrite your narrative, rather than asking yourself "If . . . ?" begin to ask yourself "How . . . ?"

I Am Not a Yoga Teacher

It was a Wednesday evening at our yoga studio, and I was looking forward to teaching one of the most popular classes on our schedule. It was called the Art of Vinyasa. It was one of my favourite classes to teach, and it was usually packed with some of our most committed and regular practitioners. The room was always magic, with forty to fifty people moving and breathing together in absolute grace. With an emphasis on the intimacy of breath and movement, it was almost as if those fifty bodies became one collective body that barely disturbed the air as we moved. The phenomenon was beautiful and sometimes brought tears to my eyes.

This Wednesday, however, was not the same. Our studio had been struggling with some changes that affected the availability of parking and significantly impacted our attendance. In addition, our landlord had increased our rent a few months prior, and the pressures associated with the business side of our yoga studio were apparent.

I walked into the practice room that afternoon and was somewhat taken aback to see that our usual number had been reduced to twelve people. I tried to tell myself that maybe there was traffic, but I knew why the room was empty. The parking situation had made it highly inconvenient for practitioners, and we had no control over it. As usual, I proceeded to guide the class and tried my best not to reveal my concern or wonder, but my mind was running a fear-driven racket. "Why is the class so small? Where is everyone? This is it: we are going to have to close the studio. We won't be able to pay rent. What about our teachers? What if I can't teach yoga any more? What am I going to do with my life?"

During the first half of that class, I was overcome with worry owing to all that was threatening our yoga studio and my identity as a yoga teacher. My attachment to that identity and the narrative that went along with it, in that moment, caused me unnecessary suffering and limited me from seeing any other possibilities for myself beyond teaching yoga.

Then there was a moment when I was able to take a few breaths, settle the negative spiral of thoughts that overcame me, and remembered that I was not a yoga teacher; it just happened to be what I did at that point in time. As much as I loved teaching yoga, I refused to allow my identity as a yoga instructor to define me. What I truly identified with was my commitment to being a better human being, to remembering what it means to embody love, and to supporting others on that journey in any way I could. Whatever shape that happened to take was irrelevant. Whether through teaching yoga, as an author, inspirational speaker, friend, or even falling to my knees and being overcome by humbling moments of weakness; my identity and narrative at any point in time are mine to write. Fortunately, I am still fulfilling my identity through the teaching of yoga, but I will no longer allow any narrative to define me or limit my possibilities, not even the ones that set my heart on fire.

Rewriting the Narratives

Our lives are one big, intimately woven, and ongoing series of narratives. We adopt social narratives about the world and use them to shape the personal narratives we write about everyone else. Then we use those narratives to discover where we fit in and write narratives about ourselves and who we think we are in relation to everything else.

As we navigate this constant web of influences and agendas, we must question all of these narratives, even the ones we write ourselves. We will identify narratives we don't align with and rewrite some of them; we will also embrace and feed the narratives that serve us. However, it's essential to note that any version of who we thought we were and what we once believed can change; in fact, it should change. Acknowledging that these narratives exist is only half the battle; to correct the prejudices, misinformation, and mistakes of the past, we have no choice but to rewrite them. The pen is in your hand – it always was.

THE NARRATIVES THAT BLIND US

Chapter 7: Questions for You

◇ What are some of the social narratives you have been told and believed without questioning? Do you feel aligned with these narratives? Why? Or why not?

◇ How do these social narratives influence your life?

◇ Can you recall instances where you created narratives about individuals or situations based on an experience or assumption without taking the time to understand?

◇ How did these personal narratives influence your relationship with these individuals?

◇ What self-narratives have you chosen to believe, and how do they limit you?

◇ Who do you dream of becoming, and how does your narrative of yourself need to change for that to happen?

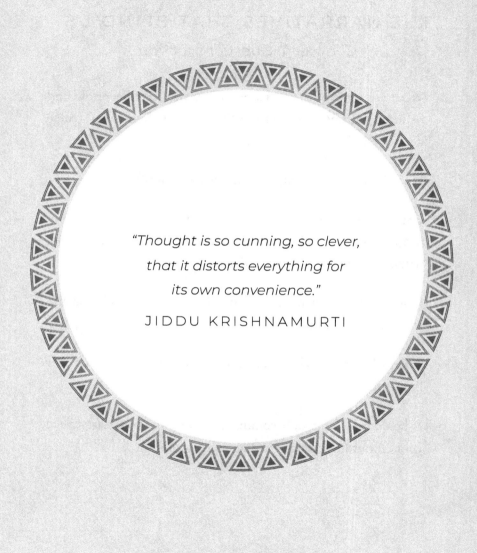

"*Thought is so cunning, so clever,
that it distorts everything for
its own convenience.*"

JIDDU KRISHNAMURTI

Accountability beyond Convenience

What if I asked you to list everything that feels out of alignment in your life, relationships, our society, and the world? I'm talking about everything from personal relationships and social culture to more significant humanitarian and global issues. In other words, this list can include everything from your spouse peeing on the toilet seat, Uncle Bob's addiction problem, the depression of a friend, and the ignorance of your boss, to consumerism, corporate responsibility, political corruption, global hunger, pandemics, oppression, inequality, and our environmental crisis. This list identifies everyone and everything that you feel requires some aspect of healing, attention, or reform.

For some of us, this might already be a long list, but it wouldn't make sense to identify problems if we didn't make an effort to suggest solutions.

That's the bonus. You also get to write a list of potential solutions to all these issues and how we might try to address them. Whether it be someone's personal transformation, social reform, or global issues, how would you envision and activate this roadmap of reform? Where would you start?

Not to worry, I am not actually asking you to write this list. However, I can't help but wonder how many of us would identify how we might be unintentionally contributing to these problems or, more importantly, where we could be part of the solutions. I am not talking about starting a riot, creating policy change, hosting interventions, or marching in the streets. Well, maybe sometimes. What I am speaking to, though, is the personal choices we make, the lifestyles we choose, how we show up in our relationships, and our ability to respond to life consciously while understanding our impact.

Accountability indicates that we are willing to acknowledge our mistakes, our disconnect, our narratives, and the ways we have contributed to the misalignments of our world. It means accepting the responsibility to be part of the solution, even when it's inconvenient for us to do so.

Playing it Safe

At some point in our lives I believe we have all dreamed of living on the edge, pushing the boundaries of what is expected, and tasting freedom, even if just for a moment. Life can become a little monotonous and stagnant as we find ourselves burdened by responsibilities and expectations; it's only natural that we would crave some adventure and freedom from time to time. It could be putting a million dollars on number seven, jumping out of a plane, or embarking on a spiritual pilgrimage. Maybe you might prefer to disappear on a wilderness trek, sail around the world, or sell all your possessions and go backpacking in the South Pacific. Everyone has their version of freedom, and we are all challenged and excited by different things, but the one thing required to attain any form of freedom is courage.

However, when it comes to freedom as it relates to our identity and the perception that others have of us, we often lack that courage. We claim that we don't care what opinions others have of us, but to some extent, we all desire to be understood, accepted, and appreciated. We prefer to be seen as aligned, centred, and ethical, or at least trying to be. Our egos would rather live in a place where we are favoured, respected, and appear to have it together. This is a comfortable space where we do not risk being judged or criticized and a place where we are not "in the wrong".

This freedom I am referring to is the readiness to own our mistakes, be seen in an unfavourable light, and maybe even ostracized. The voice of accountability is willing to say, "It was me, I did it and I was wrong. I could have done better." Because our identity and egos are constantly seeking to play it safe, we find that individuals hesitate to take ownership of their actions because of the judgement and repercussions that might follow. This means that accountability for wrongdoing and the responsibility to address the issues that need to change will usually be denied or deflected onto someone else.

Sometimes we accept wrongdoing but justify it as a response to someone else's wrongdoing, or accept responsibility as long as everyone else does as well. Before we know it, we're caught up in a blame game, and the general narrative is one where someone else should grow up, wake up, change their lifestyle, or do better. We're often too busy highlighting everyone else's unconscious patterns, conditioning, and agendas to have an honest look at our own. What about our emotional baggage, lack of support, continuous judgement, and shaming, or our lifestyle, conveniences, and narratives? Why is it always someone else?

In the case of social issues, it's always easier for us to attribute fault to the system, our leadership, a set of circumstances, or a group of individuals. That way, we don't acknowledge accountability and don't have to risk the repercussions of pointing the finger at anyone else directly. It's like sitting on the sidelines, in the comfort of our couches, and yelling at everyone on the playing field about what's going wrong and how they should fix it. Sometimes we manage to gather the courage to admit a general sense of accountability around a social issue, but avoid identifying anything specific, so that nothing within our convenient lives has to change. There are even times when we flirt with accountability and recognize that we can contribute to the necessary change, but it's just not the right time. *It's never the right time.* Unfortunately, playing the blame game and flirting with accountability rarely changes anything.

Accountability requires the commitment to take ownership of our mistakes and a willingness to do things differently, or at least genuinely to try. It calls for us to step into the spotlight and admit our misunderstandings, conditioning, unconscious actions, and even sometimes our ill intent. Accountability does not await accusation or judgement before stepping forward; it constantly reflects on how we can do better and commits to trying. Being accountable calls for the courage to embody freedom that is not attached to our image or identity. A freedom that is willing to be wrong, a freedom that is willing to be criticized, and freedom that makes our previous ideas of living on the edge appear rather dull.

The Maths of Accountability

There are social filters placed on accountability that hinder us from understanding its fundamental place and role in our society. You see, while we demand accountability of others, the primary function of accountability should never be shaming anyone, or retribution and punishment for their mistakes. This very association of accountability with wrongdoing and punishment could be why it is lacking. Being wrong makes us feel judged, diminishes our self-worth, and in many ways, threatens our acceptance and security. It is not surprising that we are resistant to taking accountability.

While there are acts of wrongdoing that call for disciplinary action, what if we altered our general perspective of accountability and saw it as a tool of growth and transformation rather than something surrounded by shame that threatened punishment? Rather than viewing accountability in a negative light, what if we simply thought of it as an acknowledgment of how we could have done better? There are always ways we could have contributed more positively, responded differently, or had a little more empathy and understanding of a situation. Maybe there were times when our actions were self-serving and caused harm to someone else; moments when we reacted emotionally and should have walked away; or instances when we could have been more truthful and courageous. There are always ways we could have done better and there is no shame in that; it is part of the human curriculum.

> The primary function of accountability should never be shaming anyone, or retribution and punishment for their mistakes.

Some of you may be resistant to this comparison, but let's look at accountability through the lens of a maths problem. We didn't always know how to add, subtract, divide, and solve equations; some of us might claim that we still don't. Imagine your teacher giving you an equation to solve, and you just can't seem to get it. Rather than berating you for getting it wrong, she takes the time to explain what you may have missed. Suddenly, with this new perspective, the equation takes another form, and the solution becomes evident. You feel empowered, your understanding has expanded, and now you are more equipped to take on the world of maths. The journey of getting it wrong, learning, understanding, and then discovering the answer is something to celebrate. Because you were not shamed, ridiculed, or punished by that teacher, the next time you are stuck on a maths problem, you will run to her willingly and say, "I don't understand. I got it wrong. What did I miss?"

I can't help but notice that accountability in our everyday lives is far less accessible. You might think that a maths problem is a little different from the situations we encounter as we navigate our relationships and our lives, and you would be right. However, if we continue to threaten every mistake and act of wrongdoing with shame, ridicule, and various forms of punishment, accountability and the potential growth that comes from it will remain scarce.

The difference between our approach to life and that maths problem is that we would approach the maths problem with an empty cup, humble and aware that we have much to learn. Unfortunately, and possibly unconsciously, most of us tend to approach life as if we are supposed to have it all figured out or have something to prove. The thing is that if we knew everything and had it all figured out, we simply would not be in our bodies. You would not be here!

The readiness to be accountable requires us to have an honest look at any situation and ask, "How have I possibly contributed to this problem? What needs to change, and how can I be part of that shift?" When we reflect on the impact of our choices and our reaction to the world around us, we discover the areas of our lives where we can do better and our potential to be part of the solution.

Once we accept more accountability, we must create a safe space for others to do the same. This means being grateful when someone takes accountability and celebrating their growth instead of punishing them and drowning them in guilt. In making accountability more accessible and nurturing a society that encourages individual growth and emotional development, we might just diminish the occurrence of acts that require punishment and retribution.

Connecting the Dots

Our lack of accountability is not always conscious; sometimes we simply have trouble connecting the dots. To imagine that our actions could affect someone else's experience of life, social inequality, or global issues seems almost ridiculous.

In the past, I've bought beverages in plastic bottles and food in single-use containers for convenience, even though I knew it contributed to environmental issues. I just didn't think I made a difference. There have been times when I used my connections to skip the line and bypass procedures because I didn't think it impacted anyone else. I had things to do and business to attend to; I just failed to realize that everyone else did as well. I have parked illegally because I figured it was just for a few minutes and wasn't a big deal. I have withheld the truth and remained silent to avoid reactions and conflict. I have unconsciously made individuals feel judged, ostracized, or neglected because they held an opposing opinion. I have been blinded by my conditioning, been emotionally reactive, and said and done things that caused others suffering and pain.

There are moments when our conveniences, privileges, and social filters cloud our perception with a subtle self-absorption that blinds us to our impact on society. Sometimes it's hard to imagine "little you" and your choices impacting the world, but that is a convenient and self-limiting belief that frees us of responsibility. As we noted in chapter 2, there are about seven billion "little yous", so consider that when you make a specific choice or decide it's okay for you to do something, you are also saying it is okay for everyone else to do it. If that does not ring true for you, maybe you believe that you are unique, and your circumstances, situation, or experiences allow you an exemption to do and say things that others should not. It is true that there are individuals whose circumstances are unique and call for exemptions and allowances; most of us, though, are simply unable to see beyond our own convenience. I believe that it is not our self-centredness or indifference that blinds us to the impact of our actions, but our disconnect and ignorance.

In 2019 the Amazon rainforest was on fire and social media was flooded with viral posts concerning global wildfires and the climate crisis. Thousands of people posted about the situation and ranted about environmental tragedies on their social media feeds, and some individuals from my extended community joined the fight to give the movement a voice.

> Our growth and conscious evolution await in the things we could have done and said differently; they live in the areas of our lives where we should have done better.

But then I saw those very same individuals sitting at a restaurant with Styrofoam takeout containers and three plastic bottles of water on the table. Single-use containers, such as Styrofoam and plastic bottles, are significant contributors to environmental issues. I do not doubt that those individuals cared about their environmental impact. I just don't think they were able to connect the dots and see how they were contributing to the problem. They were too busy blaming the "System" – big business and poor leadership – to acknowledge their accountability, however small that might appear to be.

There have been countless occasions when I have held my head in my hands and wanted to curl up in a ball, overcome with shame at the realization of my disconnect. It's easy to speak of the alignment and perspectives that resonate with a better world, but the embodiment of them is a work in progress and requires introspection. Sure, it's important to acknowledge our achievements and celebrate the good we are doing, but our growth and conscious evolution await in the things we could have done and said differently; they live in the areas of our lives where we should have done better.

Accountability can be harsh, but once we embark on the journey of self-reflection, it is fundamentally important to remember our humanness. We will make mistakes. We may repeat those mistakes, sometimes out of habit and sometimes out of convenience. When faced with this reality, remember that self-judgement and pity will not change the world; empathy, understanding, and accountability will.

Connecting the dots requires us to look at the intricacies of our actions, conversations, choices, and relationships, not just everyone else's. We must find the courage to look beyond our filters of convenience and see where we can contribute to possible solutions and support necessary change, even if we don't feel we are part of the problem. If not, our call for change is just a trend dressed in pretty words.

The Passive Plea

Sometimes we claim that we see both sides of a situation or social issue without indicating a way forward. We avoid personal accountability by being neutral. This way, we can remain passive and don't have to rock the boat by taking sides or challenging our normal. While the passive approach can be disguised as understanding, it can sometimes be cowardice and convenience.

Any fundamental change in our society and lives will likely be inconvenient for us or someone else. It may even directly challenge their way of life or their livelihood. Individuals may feel personally attacked because socially we have developed a mindset that siding with one opinion or practice implies that the other is wrong. Our sense of identity can't stand to be wrong. With that said, if we are not careful, our passivity may reinforce the idea that everything is ok as it is. It denies that anything is out of alignment and fails to acknowledge any need for a solution.

It may not feel right to label an opinion, view, or approach as "wrong", but we must ask ourselves if it is the best way forward. In this case, replacing the idea of "being wrong" with the understanding of something "not serving us at this time" would be extremely powerful.

Of course, we must also clarify who that "us" refers to. Does it only serve the "us" represented by our inner circle, our families, our friends, or is that "us" an inclusive, greater collective? I do not imply that we cannot make choices that benefit or care for our personal satisfaction and inner circles. However, if those choices are only beneficial to the comfort of our inner circle while detrimental to others, this calls for something to change.

How Dare We Not

You may be tempted to buy into that "little ole me" narrative that says your actions don't and can't make any difference. We've seen how powerful the mind is and if you believe this narrative, it will greatly influence your reality and perspective of the world, but it is a convenient and self-limiting delusion. It implies that you are separate and allows you to play small. There is no "little ole me". There is a ginormous collective *WE* and everything you do impacts that collective. Suddenly, that one plastic bottle, that one homeless person we could have fed, that one excessive purchase, that one apology, or that one act of forgiveness – it all expands and begins to take shape collectively. You are always part of the change that needs to happen. You are always part of the solution. It is time for us to accept accountability – not because we are wrong, but because we can do better.

Acknowledging our connectivity to the world around us and the responsibility that comes with it is not an easy load to carry. I'm often asked if there are days when I wake up and feel disheartened, disconnected, defeated, and question whether this human experience is even something I want to be a part of. The answer is yes. There are days when I look at what is happening in our world and simply would rather not be a part of it. There is oppression, inhumanity, genocide, environmental disregard, poverty, discrimination, the lust for money and power, pandemics, corruption, and starvation. People are being exploited, suffering, and dying unnecessarily every day. Then you can add bills to pay, mortgages, responsibilities, expectations, along with inflation and the rising cost of living.

There are days when it becomes overwhelming, and I think there is no way out of what appears to be the descending spiral of humanity; maybe I'll just disappear. I have never thought of taking my own life, but I have contemplated walking away. Going to live on a secluded island with no communication, media, news, or heartbreak. Today, I write this as a forty-year-old bachelor with no kids, and believe me, it isn't that difficult for me to disappear. Besides leaving my loved ones behind, saying goodbye to society would be easy.

For some individuals, their way of disappearing is dismissal and avoidance. It sometimes makes life easier to bear if we simply don't turn on the news or pay too much attention to what's happening around us. We can create our tiny bubbles of reality, convenience, and leisure without being burdened by anything outside that bubble.

Another avenue of avoidance is the plea of the empath: we claim to be overly sensitive or too empathetic, and that the state of the world affects us deeply. We use this plea to justify our withdrawal, and it may be true for some individuals (who am I to say?) but it appears that everyone these days is claiming to be an empath. I know this approach well; I see it among my friends and community, and have also flirted with these methods of avoidance myself. Fortunately, now I know a little better and it usually isn't long before I hear the words, "How dare you?"

They were words I first heard from Seane Corn while attending leadership training with an organization called Off the Mat into the World. Essentially, these were the words that helped me acknowledge my privilege, along with the many conveniences, luxuries, and blessings that fill my life. Whenever the world begins to get overwhelmingly heavy or daunting, I allow myself to feel it momentarily; then I remind myself that I can make a difference, even in the smallest ways. With all that I have been given, how dare I not at least try? The monologue in my head goes something like this:

No matter how heavy it seems at times

No matter how big the hurdle

No matter how long the fight

No matter how many generations of misinformation we have to undo

No matter how many hearts we have to change

No matter how many doubts we have to overcome or conveniences we must give up

No matter if our names are forgotten or our efforts go unnoticed

No matter how sick our society appears or how damaged our planet

No matter how many wrongs we have to forgive or souls we have to stir

No matter how many shadows we have to face or mistakes we must own

No matter how many lifetimes it takes to remember who we are

To lose ourselves in love

How dare we not try at every opportunity, with every breath, in every way we can?

ACCOUNTABILITY BEYOND CONVENIENCE

Chapter 8: Questions for You

◇ What are some of the situations you would like to influence in your personal life? How would you like to shift them, and how can you facilitate that without placing blame or judgement?

◇ What are some of the more significant issues in our society and our world that need to be addressed? Where and how can you contribute more consciously?

◇ Have you attempted to punish someone for their wrongdoing instead of explaining how they have made you feel or impacted others negatively? How could you have made accountability more accessible?

◇ Do you tend to take a passive stand or perspective in situations? Can you recall some of these situations and why you chose passivity?

◇ Right now, where and how are you personally willing to be part of the solution? This is your commitment to at least try your best to _____ (fill in the blank).

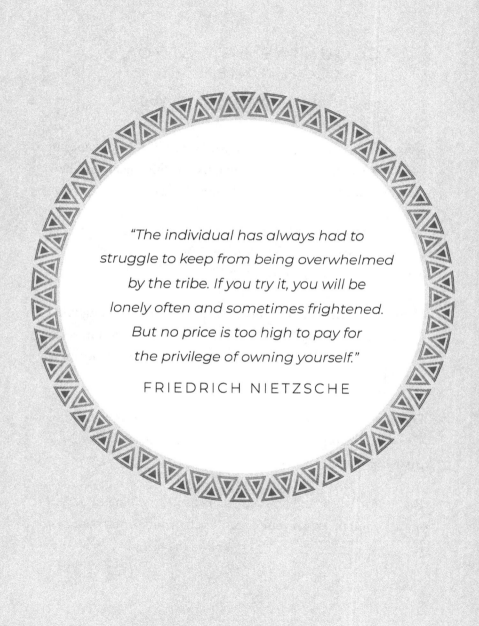

"The individual has always had to struggle to keep from being overwhelmed by the tribe. If you try it, you will be lonely often and sometimes frightened. But no price is too high to pay for the privilege of owning yourself."

FRIEDRICH NIETZSCHE

Authenticity and Corruption

We live in a copycat society where we politely mimic current fashions and trends, aim to meet expectations, and try our best not to ruffle too many feathers. When referencing authenticity, I am referring to how we portray ourselves in the world. Are we genuine in our actions and words, or do we simply say and do what we believe everyone wants to hear?

Authenticity is the ability to be genuine, real, and truthful, regardless of social resistance or reaction, and that begins with introspection. Taking the time to understand how we truly feel about any situation, ideology, or perspective – and why. It would be impossible to be genuine if we didn't understand our sentiments, emotions, and opinions. Without introspection we could find ourselves being true to someone else's ideas and beliefs, adopting their views, and playing out a narrative that uses us as a pawn. We often don't even realize we are inauthentic because our constant desire to be accepted has led to the repetition of social norms and ideas that have made inauthenticity normal. Authenticity begins by acknowledging how we genuinely feel about any situation, what we believe, and why.

Our society is made up of individuals, and each individual is in direct relationship with the greater society. I emphasize this relationship because, while we are a product of that society, we also create and shape it. The influence of that relationship goes both ways. It would not be far-fetched to say that any corruption or misalignment in our world has its roots in individual belief systems and behaviours. It is tempting to point fingers and call names, but unfortunately, that means you and me. This is part of the accountability we spoke about in the last chapter. The quality of our relationships and the integrity surrounding them (or lack thereof) collectively shape our society. It may seem like a long shot, but I am suggesting that we are contributing to corruption if we are not being authentic in our everyday lives.

The Right to be Authentic

It's important to acknowledge that being authentic does not necessarily speak to someone's morals, ethics, or integrity. While we often associate authenticity with morality and good character, that is not necessarily the case. Everyone has the right to be authentic, regardless of their opinions or beliefs. This may be hard to accept in many cases because we can all identify ideologies that we oppose and opinions that we feel should not have a voice. But would it be ethical to censor an individual's right to be authentic?

The power of words and ideas can ignite human emotions, inspire revolution, rattle belief systems, and unify or divide us. There are ideologies whose intentions I question and whose perspectives I might view as egotistical, self-centred, and delusional. For me, these are the belief systems that feed division, inequality, injustice, and oppression. Knowing how powerful words and ideas can be, I have often struggled in my consideration of "free speech". I believe that some of these ideas poison our society, and part of me would rather they not have a voice and be buried forever.

However, the reality is that these sentiments and perspectives do exist, and as much as I wish I could snap my fingers and make them disappear, that probably isn't going to happen anytime soon. Even if I could, having them suddenly vanish might not necessarily be a good thing in the long run. To remove the voice of ideologies that we consider harmful or out of alignment would be comparable to covering up the symptoms of an illness and pretending it did not exist. If we have any intention of healing the misalignments of our society, we must create space to allow these ideologies an authentic voice so that we can address them.

Whether or not you believe that a specific perspective serves humanity, the individual who holds that belief considers it right and true. While this does not justify or condone hateful, oppressive, or inhumane ideologies, condemning and punishing them without understanding where they come from is only a temporary solution. Imagine what it would be like if you are muted and told all those thoughts, emotions, ideas, and opinions that you consider true are wrong and unacceptable. You would then be made to feel delusional, offered no outlet for expression, and no attempt would be made to help you process your sentiments or understand why they might be misaligned. Is that not a form of oppression? I imagine that it would fuel resentment and trauma, leading to an ongoing domino effect of division and disconnect.

Furthermore, what if some of these ideas and opinions, while first considered radical and alternative, were a form of social medicine?

> The healing of our society must include the healing of toxic belief systems and those who hold them. The right to be authentic is essential to the collective healing process.

Consider the thousands of freedom fighters and revolutionaries who shattered many misalignments and changed our world with their alternative counter-culture beliefs. Who has the right to decide what should be allowed an authentic voice and what should not? Who determines what serves our collective society and what doesn't? The same views we resist might reveal how our current perspectives could be limited, biased, or self-centred.

While we may resist the general idea that every ideology and opinion deserves an authentic voice, consider that humanity, in the collective sense, extends far beyond one lifetime. In other words, something is happening that is more significant than our individual experience, lifetime, and even our generation. There are many things that we, as a collective consciousness, need to experience and learn in order to heal and evolve, and it will take time. There are ways in which we need to grow that will be uncomfortable and sometimes painful. The healing of our society must include the healing of toxic belief systems and those who hold them. The right to be authentic is essential to the collective healing process. If we do not create space for the illnesses of our society to show their symptoms, it would be impossible to treat them.

That Skirt and those Boots

We are all influenced by our friends and social circles to an extent, but I was never one to follow the crowd if it didn't feel right. My friends and family never really made me think that I needed to. Regardless of how different my views or opinions were, they always gave me space to be authentic. They challenge me in the ways I need to be challenged, invite me to question my narratives of truth, and above all, allow me the freedom to be authentic. Without them, I would not be the person I am today – not even close.

Growing up, it didn't even dawn on me that inauthenticity was an option. I dressed a little differently, danced to a rhythm that no one else seemed to hear, and generally didn't care much what anyone thought of it. Growing up in Trinidad, where alcohol is a pillar of social life from early adolescence, I had chosen the unthinkable path of sobriety. When asked how I managed to navigate life in Trinidad and Tobago without drinking, I again give much credit to my inner circle of friends. Sure, the occasional joke or subtle remarks made it known that having a drink was always an option, but I never felt any ridicule that threatened my acceptance. My friends would even stand up for me if I were pressured by anyone who didn't understand. I saw the world through a different lens, and it was okay, at least to the people who surrounded me.

There were always some people who didn't take the time to understand or have a conversation in an attempt to. They would create narratives about who I was and what I believed simply from how I dressed, danced, and anything else that fed their story. It was never something I took personally, and I knew that if anyone took the time to have a conversation, they would get it. Honestly, I have even looked back at pictures from my late teens and early twenties and wondered what exactly I could have been thinking. I recently joked with one of my lifelong friends that I appreciate how much he loves me because he stood by my side all those years while I made outrageous fashion statements. With his smartass smirk, he said that it only made him look more attractive in comparison.

As an adult there have been times when it has been challenging to be authentic, and then there were other times when it could have been seen as downright inappropriate. I clearly recall one night that fell into the categories of both. I had been invited to a twenty-first birthday party, and the fancy printed invitation stated the dress code was semi-formal. It wouldn't be the first time I had bent the rules of what would be considered acceptable, but that night the rebel within me decided to push the boundaries of my circles a little more than usual. It so happened that I was about to meet my match.

I carefully selected my favourite bohemian-style skirt for the occasion. It was long, patterned, comfortable, and my mom often joked that she might borrow it. I think it was her way of subtly saying, "Troy, are you losing your mind?" Usually, if I were going to wear a long skirt, I would at least wear sandals, hoping that it might be somewhat more acceptable if I kept it casual. However, as this event was semi-formal, I decided to put on my military-style boots and an embroidered Indian-style kurta to top it off. Adding to the spectacle was my straggly, shoulder-length, sun-bleached hair, along with enough jewellery to make someone wonder if I had just robbed a store. I understand that this could have been normal among the hippie culture of the 60s in the US, but this was Trinidad, it was 2002, and this party was pretty conventional and what one might call "uptown".

The faces at the party were mostly familiar except for a few con-cerned parents on the sidelines, probably praying that I didn't ask their daughter – or their son – to dance. There were reactions of all kinds. Some of my friends thought it was highly inappropriate, some used it as entertainment, and to my inner circle of friends, it was simply Troy being Troy. I recall a few occasions when someone would move away from me if they found themselves standing too close with no one else around. I assumed it was fear of association, but I never allowed myself to be bothered.

I was standing with some friends among the crowd of slacks, button-down shirts, fashionable dresses, and high heels when I saw another epic display of authenticity across the dance floor. His name was Jamie, and I didn't know him all that well, but we had graced similar social circles for years. Jamie had somewhat of a bad-boy reputation and an image that matched. Even though Jamie fitted in, with his slacks and button-down shirt, he clearly wanted to ensure that he maintained his edge. On the top of his freshly shaved head were two new tattoos: flaming blue horns began at his hairline and blazed their way back as if he was a charging bull. I wondered if Jamie might regret that decision in the future, but I also thought, "Wow, that kind of commitment takes some serious courage."

Later that night, I saw Jamie walking across the dance floor and couldn't help but notice the intricacies of his tattoo, and it was impressive. We had never spoken much, but would usually share passing glances and nods of recognition. This time there was no passing glance or nod. Jamie locked my eyes and headed straight towards me with his bad-boy stagger. He was generally a bit intimidating, but now, with those horns on his head charging toward me, he took on a whole new persona. If it weren't for the subtle smile on his face, I would have probably been more concerned.

Jamie arrived in front of me, looked me up and down, then stepped in close enough so I could hear him over the blaring sound system. As he put his hand on my shoulder and leaned into me, he said, "Troy, I have real love and respect for you, but the only thing in this party more fucked up than the horns on my head is that skirt and those boots." That was it. He smiled, gave me a nudge along with his usual nod, and staggered off.

It wasn't anything I ever thought I would have someone tell me (I'm pretty sure that strange and unique combination of words had never been spoken otherwise, nor will it ever). I was just happy he didn't kick me in my head or set my skirt on fire. While I didn't realize it then, looking back on the exchange, Jamie had no intention of insulting me; it was an act of respect and acknowledgment. Jamie respected that I dared to walk my path, make my own choices, and would not do something simply because it was expected. Jamie understood this was a statement. It was a statement that said I could think for myself and act in alignment with my beliefs, regardless of how society felt about it. While Jamie and I had come from very different backgrounds and may have had different perspectives on the world, it was the same statement he was making with his flaming blue horns.

The desire to express oneself authentically is instinctive and present in every individual. It is social conditioning that causes us to question how we authentically feel and attempts to influence our actions. The reactions and responses of others communicate what is deemed acceptable, favourable, and even punishable. This is not a bad thing: this dynamic is essential in shaping the moral boundaries of society and dictates what actions are appropriate or harmful. At the same time, it is fundamental to create a society where individuals are free to express themselves without the fear of judgement or alienation, and even challenge social boundaries in the name of collective betterment.

Reprogramming

In chapter 7, we visited the general concept of narratives and considered the impact of accepting social norms without questioning them. However, it's not only narratives and belief systems that we unconsciously adopt, but also behaviours. These behavioural patterns influence how we react, respond, and communicate. They become part of our programming and are communicated by the actions of those around us. In other words, we will unconsciously repeat the behaviours we are exposed to, until, of course, we begin to question them.

Some of the behaviours we pick up in many ways carry the emotional baggage, trauma, and disconnect of our loved ones and communities. They might include self-centredness, our response to being wronged, the manner in which we speak to people, patterns of avoidance and habitual

> It isn't just the behaviour of toxic patterns and trauma that is learned as part of our programming, but also the healing of them.

numbing, our attitude towards forgiveness and accountability, and even the manner in which we show and expect to receive love. What's beautiful, though, is that it isn't just the behaviour of toxic patterns and trauma that is learned as part of our programming, but also the healing of them. That means we have an opportunity to be part of this healing and rewrite toxic programming, but it demands authenticity and requires us to quiet the noise of our social influences.

This, of course, is not an easy task. Sometimes it means taking a step away from those influences to observe them and reflect on how they might impact our relationships. Other times, we may need to immerse ourselves in these social behaviours to understand their intentions, where they came from, and why people behave the way they do. Either way, it's important to remember that our introspection, observation, and questioning should never aim to judge or condemn but to understand and heal.

Quieting the noise of our social influences can often feel like climbing Mount Everest in full scuba gear – wetsuit, mask, tank, snorkel, and flippers. On top of all that, when we identify the toxic behaviours that need to change, authenticity calls for us to highlight and communicate the misalignments and impact of those behaviours. This is not always easy to do without offending and triggering the people we love, and you can expect an avalanche. It is essential that our communication offers alternative ways of being and outlines why they are necessary, and that we embody the behavioural changes we call for. On this note, we must acknowledge that inauthenticity also lives in our silence. If there are things we feel need to be said, communicated, or addressed, then to remain silent would be dishonest. Our commitment to authenticity does not depend on favourable or supportive reactions from our friends, co-workers, and families. That said, how we communicate our sentiments can either reveal the potential to reprogramme toxic behaviour or shut down any chance of that happening.

In challenging the norm, we risk losing friends, jobs, families, and any safety net that our circles provide. The path of authenticity can potentially leave you navigating a lonely trail with all your scuba gear while being chased by the abominable snowman. Thankfully, though, more and more people choose to walk that trail every day.

Emotional Corruption

We have all been inauthentic at some point in our lives, probably more than we would like to admit. Referring to inauthenticity as corruption may appear harsh, but let's call it as it is. What logical reasons can you imagine for saying and doing the things you don't truly align with? That you don't believe in? Maybe your life is being threatened, or you don't feel it is the right time, but more often than not, we are buying approval and acceptance, avoiding conflict, or fear ridicule. I understand that the word "corruption" may be a lot to swallow, because when we think of corruption, we think of financial kickbacks, bribes, or billions of dollars diverted to untraceable accounts. So let's butter it up a little. Rather than calling it corruption with a capital C, let's call inauthenticity a form of "emotional corruption". Don't be fooled, though; emotional corruption is just as dangerous, disguises itself in our relationships, and has become a thread within our society.

When it comes to emotional intimidation and corruption, we are often unaware that we are being inauthentic, bribed, or even offering a kickback. We say and do things to buy approval, support, acceptance, and even love. We use these tactics to avoid criticism, conflict, and even to buy silence. I can only imagine that it came from generations of threatening punishment and offering rewards to influence behaviour. As kids, we may have been bribed with safety and affection. As young adults, it may have been acceptance and fear of ridicule that guided us. In adulthood, it may be opportunities and inclusion. Emotional corruption comes in many forms and has found its way into various social exchanges that we consider acceptable.

As with accountability, it is essential to note that our inaction and silence can be just as corrupt as what we do or say. Sometimes we remain quiet because we don't want to risk our reputation, sponsors, or disapproval from family and friends. It could have been that one controversial post we decided not to share, a conversation we have been avoiding, or an inappropriate comment from a friend that you should have brought to their attention. While there are legitimate considerations that might influence our actions or inaction, if our choices are dependent upon or seeking approval, acceptance, or support, it could be an emotional bribe.

This reflection is not complete without turning the tables. We don't just pay these emotional bribes, but also accept them. We often use our authority, our role in our communities, and our place in relationships to discourage people from being authentic to their truth. Sometimes we even use our moods, attitude, and subtle energy to communicate disapproval, intimidate, or isolate the people in our lives. The cold shoulder, pouting, and silent treatment are all aspects of emotional corruption, and while often unconscious, they have become part of our everyday lives. If the quality of your relationships depends on your support, agreement, or opinions, then you must question the authenticity of those relationships. That questioning could reveal how some of our relationships might bear more resemblance to business deals than genuine friendships.

The Bigger Picture

The emotional corruption of our relationships slowly begins to make its way into more prominent aspects of our society, unnoticed for the most part. One example of this worth mentioning is the growing acceptance of social influencers. It is becoming increasingly acceptable for individuals to be paid for endorsements on their social media platforms. Firstly, let's note that many social media influencers genuinely endorse products and initiatives they believe in. It's an amazing avenue to give a voice to small businesses and individuals who might not be able to get that voice heard otherwise. However, there are social influencers who endorse products and services they don't believe in or are not even familiar with. If we personally promote establishments and brands whose ethics, products, and practices we are not in alignment with,

> The corruption of our politicians, our leaders, and the heads of big corporations didn't suddenly happen when they found themselves in influential roles; it has been an ongoing part of our everyday relationships and society for a long time.

in exchange for money, product, or an audience, are we not being inauthentic? Is the selling of our influence and voice any different from accepting a bribe or someone buying a vote?

The corruption of our politicians, our leaders, and the heads of big corporations didn't suddenly happen when they found themselves in influential roles; it has been an ongoing part of our everyday relationships and society for a long time. These decision-makers have now simply found themselves playing with billions of dollars, international policy and relations, and the well-being of our nations.

While addressing political and corporate corruption may appear overwhelming and beyond our reach, the good news is that emotional corruption is directly within our control. As with many misalignments in our world, the only way to dissolve emotional corruption is by identifying where we participate and contribute to it, consciously and unconsciously. When we commit to creating space in our relationships for others to be authentic without criticism, judgement, or kickbacks, we encourage them to do the same. Together, we begin to rewrite social programming.

To live authentically in our society almost guarantees that we will be ridiculed and criticized. Furthermore, while it might not be our intention, our authenticity will sometimes hurt, offend, and disappoint the people we love. I was once reminded by a dear friend that we will rock the boat if we are committed to being authentic and creating change in the world. The change we seek to create is not always systemic; much of the time, that change needs to happen on a personal level and within our social circles first. Each of us has a choice to make, and we must decide if our priority is being popular and favoured or if we are here to facilitate transformation and bring light to the darkness.

While navigating the journey of embodying and communicating your authenticity, remember that your words are mighty. Speak your truth but be careful not to disregard or judge the feelings and opinions of others. As author and astrologer Antero Alli once shared, "Truth without compassion is cruelty."

AUTHENTICITY AND CORRUPTION

Chapter 9: Questions for You

◇ Can you identify some of the times that you have been inauthentic? Why did you feel you needed to be?

◇ What are some of the ways you have consciously or unconsciously discouraged others from being authentic? How did you use your influence to manipulate their opinions and actions?

◇ Are there any opinions or ideologies you feel do not deserve a voice? What are they? Why? Can you see any benefit in allowing them that voice?

◇ Are there any current situations or relationships in your life that make it hard for you to be authentic? What are they?

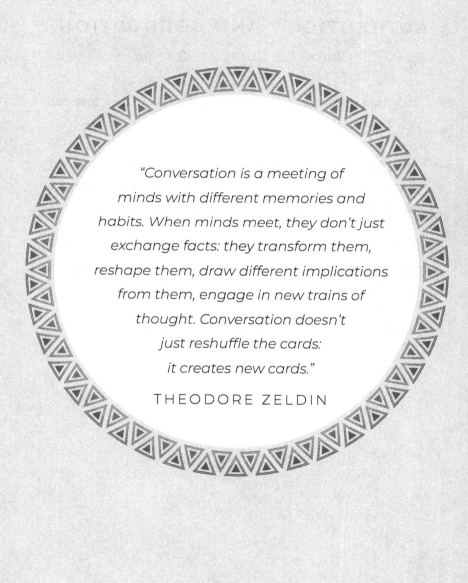

"Conversation is a meeting of minds with different memories and habits. When minds meet, they don't just exchange facts: they transform them, reshape them, draw different implications from them, engage in new trains of thought. Conversation doesn't just reshuffle the cards: it creates new cards."

THEODORE ZELDIN

Transformative Conversation

have walked away from many conversations with my head in my hands, my heart on the floor, and feeling defeated because I should have known better. In these situations, I allowed myself to be overcome by emotion and blinded by my commitment to the cause. My passion and rigidity, while well-intentioned, diminished any chances of real conversation or the transformation that could have resulted. Looking back at those conversations now, I can't help but wonder what I was thinking. What did I think would happen after accusing someone of wrongdoing or ignorance, attacking their beliefs, and essentially telling them it's their fault? Then on top of that, indicating what they should do, how they should feel, and what they should believe?

While authentic and transformative conversation is indeed an art,

> A conversation of the heart not only changes someone's opinion but shifts something within them and changes them forever.

that sounds a lot more like the art of war than anything resembling a wholesome and heartfelt conversation.

Conversations of the heart seek to understand, consider different perspectives, and emphasize sharing and growth as the primary agenda. Unfortunately, conversations where there are differences of opinion often aim to change someone's mind, focus on having someone act according to our wishes, admit we are right, or to get an apology. That conversation is driven by ego and may create a temporary change of mind; however, a conversation of the heart not only changes someone's opinion but shifts something within them and changes them forever.

Communication and Conversation

We are continuously communicating with one another, through spoken words, body language, energetic exchanges, art, music, and every imaginable form of media. Our methods of communication are diverse, and thanks to technology, messages can now cross borders at the speed of light and be received by future generations with a series of clicks and searches. This book, for example, is my method of communicating with you right now, but in fifty years, these words could just as easily be read by someone who hasn't even been born yet. While all conversations can fall under the umbrella of communication, not all communication is conversation. Consider that conversations are real-time and also include telephone and video calls, but there is an element of tone, emotion, and even body language that cannot be communicated through the world of text, emojis, abbreviations, and blue ticks.

While all methods of communication are expressions of the things we think and feel, they are not all conversations. The conversations I am referring to are spoken words and verbal exchanges between individuals where we share sentiments and information, discuss ideas, express our emotions, and offer perspectives. They are more personal and intimate than other forms of communication, but it's also important to note that conversations don't always have to be long or intense. Sometimes the most impactful conversations can consist of brief social exchanges with absolute strangers.

Subtle Opportunities

The lady must have been in her late fifties and appeared somewhat confused. She had walked through the doors of our yoga studio with some uncertainty and was greeted by our studio manager, Jade. After welcoming the lady and discovering that she was looking for the business next door, Jade redirected her, and invited her to come back and attend a class or relax among the community. However, before closing the conversation, Jade couldn't help but compliment the lady's beautiful eyes and stunning appearance. After what appeared to be a moment of disbelief, the lady smiled, said, "Thank you," and hurried awkwardly out of the door.

Overhearing the exchange, I told Jade I felt the lady would definitely be back soon, but I didn't even finish my sentence before the doors swung open, and the lady marched back in. This time she was wearing unmistakable confidence. She firmly placed her bag on the counter, looked Jade in the eyes, and with a few teardrops creeping down her cheek, she quietly said, "That was the first compliment I have received in over twenty years. I just wanted to let you know how much it meant to me. Thank you."

Jade's simple compliment impacted that lady's life in a beautiful way, but what may be less obvious is the impact that exchange had on Jade's. Some years later, while writing this book, I asked Jade if she remembered that interaction and her reply revealed an entirely new perspective.

"That changed my life," she said. "Ever since that day, I have tried to make an extra effort to tell everyone something nice. No matter what."

Not only did that simple exchange impact that lady in ways we might never understand, but it reminded Jade of the opportunities she had every day to impact people positively, even in the smallest of ways.

These conversations happen every day, and the truth is that if the lady had not found the courage to come back into the studio, it would have appeared to be just another casual, superficial exchange. Consider that every interaction and every conversation is a gift. When we connect with someone, even briefly, we are given an opportunity to influence their journey and share in their lives. How you decide to use that opportunity and if you choose to unwrap that gift is up to you. Unfortunately, many of these gifts remain unwrapped, underappreciated, and often unnoticed.

Our words are sometimes more powerful than our actions. When it comes to our conversations, one word to the right person at the right time could change their lives; it could also change yours.

Sometime during my late teens, I came across the idea that words had vibrations and decided that I would greet everyone with the word "love". I couldn't imagine any better vibration to bring into the world, and it wasn't long before "love" became the word I would use to say hello as well as goodbye. The impact this was having didn't occur to me until years later, when I overheard my mother ending a few of her telephone conversations in the same way.

Then there was a conversation when it truly hit home in a whole different way. I was in Whistler, Canada, supporting one of my teachers, Ryan Leier, at a yoga festival, and it was time to check out of my hotel. I contacted the front desk to request a wake-up call and a cab for my early-morning flight. The concierge said he would call me back to confirm, and as usual, I ended that phone call with: "Love." A few minutes later, the phone rang, and it was the concierge confirming my taxi for 5 a.m. Again, I closed that conversation with a quick "Love." That's when the concierge, whom I had never met, with a smile in his voice, replied, "I love you too."

While I can't tell you the impact my "love" had on that concierge in our first conversation, his up-levelling of my "love" reminded me that even one word can influence someone's life. It said that he had felt appreciated and acknowledged; even without seeing his face or knowing his name, my brief conversation with that concierge is etched into my heart.

Your words can lift people up, inspire them, and make them feel appreciated, but they can also bring people down, feed their insecurities, and leave them feeling judged. Sometimes a harmless joke with a friend or a comment repeated to you as a child can result in a lingering sense of insecurity, doubt, and alienation. On the flip side, there are ordinary moments of acknowledgment, encouragement, and gratitude that can give someone's life meaning. Words are vibrations, and much like love and fear, they carry a tangible resonance. Bringing more awareness and subtlety to your everyday conversations might reveal that you have more opportunities to change the world than you had previously realized.

Heart-to-Heart or Head-to-Head

Here I'm referring to the conversations in which we share the depths of our views, experiences, feelings, and opinions. Consider them heart-to-heart or sometimes, unfortunately, head-to-head conversations. We've all had them. These exchanges get us emotional, challenge our opinions, and even rattle our sense of identity. While these conversations have real potential for growth and transformation, they can also create narratives of otherness, separation, rivalry, hurt, and even betrayal.

What often occurs in these conversations is that we identify so strongly with our opinions or feelings that we find ourselves blinded by our emotions. As we saw in chapter 2, our opinions and ideas are part of our identity, and when they are challenged, we often feel threatened and personally attacked. Our agenda becomes the defence of our opinion, and we can find ourselves getting worked up, throwing all composure aside, and giving our peace away. Usually, it's not long before everyone involved is either emotionally triggered or has completely shut down. When this happens, the potential for growth from that conversation diminishes, along with the consideration that we may have something to learn.

> If our only agenda is to prove our point, based on what we think we know, it makes more sense to talk to ourselves.

These conversations come in various forms, and each one carries its own unique dynamic and context. Regardless, if the hope for a conversation is to create space for growth and transformation, then our desire to listen and understand one another is essential. We must be willing to put ourselves in someone's situation, understand their perspective, and feel the emotion being expressed. It is also important to note that assuming we know someone's intentions, experiences, or agenda is very different from the genuine intention to understand them. We have already seen how the mind can convince us that our assumptions are truth and fact, and if our only agenda is to prove our point, based on what we think we know, it makes more sense to talk to ourselves. A genuine desire to understand someone else's point of view requires we listen to the emotions, experiences, and intentions being conveyed, not just the words being spoken.

You would think that listening is an obvious part of any conversation, but we live in a world where everyone is talking and trying to be heard, but not many people are listening. As Stephen Covey, author of *The 7 Habits of Highly Effective People*, puts it, "People don't listen to understand. They listen to reply. The collective monologue is everyone talking, and no one is listening." If you are in a conversation, listening while simultaneously plotting your response – that is not authentic listening. Unless we listen to understand, there won't be much chance for transformation and growth to come out of any conversation. In listening to understand, we create the space to ask ourselves where someone's perspective has come from. Is there a narrative? Who does it benefit, and how? What am I missing? Why am I triggered? Through the genuine desire to understand one another and the listening that is necessary, we nurture a relationship that honours and respects everyone involved, even if we disagree and cannot find common ground.

When our only agenda, consciously or unconsciously, is to establish ourselves as right or defend our views, any possibility of understanding an opposing view or the individual who holds it is lost. Someone will always end up feeling defeated, judged, wronged, silenced, or misunderstood. This is a conversation of minds, and we are trying to change someone's mind. However, true transformation doesn't happen on a mind level; it requires a conversation of the heart. Creating a shift at a heart level truly influences an individual, their perspectives, and their approach to life. When we have conversations on a heart level, everyone leaves as a different person from the one who went into it.

Guns Down and Heart Open

Having conversations of the heart calls for us to put our guns down and stand at the frontline with our hearts in our hands. Putting our guns down means our priority is not to judge, condemn, or frame anyone as wrong. It is a gesture that says we come in peace and seek to understand an individual, their intentions, and their perspectives.

With our guns on the floor and our hearts in our hands, we may be exposed and vulnerable, but, more importantly, we become a catalyst for conversations of the heart. Exposing your heart means sharing your emotions, experiences, fears, and even weaknesses. It opens us up to potential humiliation, hurt, and defeat. However, to understand someone authentically, we must sometimes set the tone and bear it all. In our commitment to having conversations on a heart level there is no room for intimidation tactics or pretending to be anything we are not. With our hearts in our hands and guns on the floor, we create a space that encourages others to do the same.

But just because you have set the foundation for a conversation of the heart doesn't mean someone else won't pick up their guns and begin blazing. There is always a chance that someone might get triggered, and in a heartbeat, you can find yourself exposed and under attack.

You cannot control how anyone else reacts in a conversation, but you can manage your response. If you allow yourself to be triggered or pick up your guns in response to a perceived attack, everyone loses. Conversations of the heart can ruffle some feathers, and no matter what you do, sometimes they will be perceived as an attack. Regardless, remember that it is far better to maintain our bridges of communication and respect rather than burning those bridges with resentment. Without such a bridge, our potential to influence someone's perspective diminishes, along with our ability to touch their heart.

The Peacemakers

There will always be conversations where we feel resented, disheartened, frustrated, or unheard. Sometimes we manage to maintain our composure and keep our emotions in check, but then there are moments when we pull the pin on the grenade and blow that bridge of communication to pieces. Fortunately, while it may take time, bridges can be rebuilt.

This is where the Peacemakers come in. They are a little cluster of expressions that carry immense power, and while we have all come across them before, we don't always use them as authentically or as often as we should. Some of us may recognize them as the Hawaiian practice known as *Ho'oponopono*, but I imagine they have existed in many forms and cultures for centuries. By no means are they infallible solutions to every conversational battlefield, but they are versatile and, when used authentically, can usually dispel a gunfight or rebuild any bridge.

> **Thank You.** This does not only mean you are grateful or appreciative of what someone has done or said, but more importantly, you are grateful that someone is doing their best. That someone is authentic, showing up, or making space for a conversation to happen. There is always something to be thankful for, no matter the relationship. Letting someone know they are appreciated and seen can go a long way.

> **I am sorry.** This does not always have to be an acknowledgment of wrongdoing. "I'm sorry" can be an acknowledgment of the hurt we have caused, even if we feel we have acted with integrity or authenticity. "I'm sorry" can be a fresh start, a resolution to ongoing conflict, and healing of an open wound.

I forgive you. Consider that forgiving does not necessarily mean forgetting, but it does mean understanding that everyone is a product of their experiences. Someone's intentions may not have been to do wrong or hurt another deliberately, and forgiveness creates space for healing. It reminds us that if someone had known better and could have done better, they would have. Forgiveness eventually frees everyone involved from guilt, suffering, and pain.

I love you. It is essential to acknowledge that to love someone does not necessarily mean you love everything they believe in or identify with. To love someone is to see that there is a soul beyond the narrative trying to find its way home, as we all are. To love someone is to acknowledge that we all have our baggage and are committed to supporting each other on our journey. Saying "I love you" is an absolute commitment to let someone know they are not alone; that no matter what happens, they will never be alone.

> Our conversations have the power to dissolve the illusion of our differences.

The power of our conversations to transform our relationships, society, and world is undeniable. The more we create the space to listen and understand one another, the more we discover the potential for collective growth and transformation. There is only one way forward, and that is together. Our conversations have the power to dissolve the illusion of our differences.

TRANSFORMATIVE CONVERSATION

Chapter 10: Questions for You

◇ Can you recall any situations or conversations where you felt you were not being understood or heard? How did that feel? Why do you think that happened?

◇ Have you ever been so blinded by your opinions and perspectives that you failed to create the space for someone else to be heard? How could you have responded differently?

◇ Have any subtle conversations or brief exchanges moved you? What was it about them and the delivery that touched you, and how?

◇ What are some things you feel you can work on personally regarding your approach to conversations?

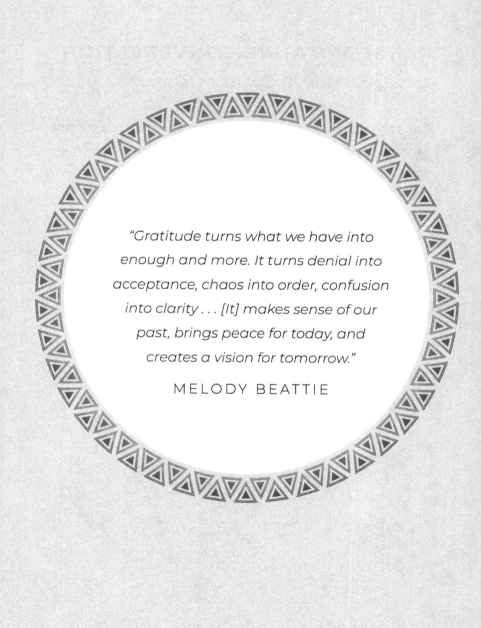

"Gratitude turns what we have into enough and more. It turns denial into acceptance, chaos into order, confusion into clarity . . . [It] makes sense of our past, brings peace for today, and creates a vision for tomorrow."

MELODY BEATTIE

The Full Circle of Gratitude

Our perspective on the human experience is a bit short-sighted, and this impacts many aspects of our lives, including our understanding of gratitude. When contemplating gratitude, we generally think of the people, things, and experiences that fulfil our desires, meet our needs, and give us a sense of security, along with all that brings us joy, laughter, and inspiration. In other words, our need for security and desire to feel safe limits our gratitude to all the things that appear favourable and pleasant: the rainbows and butterflies of life. This limited view of gratitude echoes a subconscious sense of entitlement that portrays life as nothing more than a journey of fun and games. It's almost as if we believe that life should only consist of fresh fruit, chocolate, sunny days, calm seas, and long walks on the beach.

If we take a moment to acknowledge the artistry and unexplainable intelligence that crafts our world, it seems somewhat self-centred and shallow to imagine it revolves around us *Homo sapiens*. Consider that life is like a universal school designed to teach us resilience, compassion, forgiveness and remind us what it means to love. Every time life humbled you or broke your heart could be part of the curriculum intended and designed for your evolution and development. To me it only makes sense that our lives, in some way, are also intended to facilitate our emotional and spiritual maturing.

It doesn't stop there. We are not only in school, but we are also the school; we execute the lesson plan for others. Your personal hardships could set the stage for someone else's growth. Your struggles could afford someone else the opportunity to learn compassion. Your shortcomings and mistakes might allow others to understand forgiveness, and your despair could be someone's wake-up call.

While this idea may not be easy to grasp, remember this isn't physical training, where you go to the gym to lose weight or get fit. Life is emotional and spiritual training, you are part of a larger collective body, and the work we have come to do is not as simple as washboard abs.

Life is not all rainbows and butterflies. There will be times when it feels like you are drowning in murky waters while a flying elephant shits on your head. If your perspective is short-sighted and you are looking at life through the filters of individual identity and immediate satisfaction, these murky waters will feel darker and heavier. The ability to remove those filters and approach these situations with humility and appreciation reveals their potential for growth and transformation. Genuine gratitude must go full circle in appreciating both the light and what appears at any moment as dark.

Give Thanks for Life

It was the first time I had ever set foot on African soil, and even as a white-skinned West Indian Arab, it felt like home. The resonance was tangible, and I knew that all the tales of Africa I had heard through my Rastafarian influences were true. Without any doubt, I could feel that this was where it all began. While I was tempted to join my friends on organized excursions, beach trips, and other tourist activities, I knew Africa had something else in store for me. I just wasn't sure what it was or where I would find it.

One afternoon I decided to roam the streets of Cape Town and see what it led to. I walked into a little streetside corner shop that resembled shops I had visited back home in Trinidad. From the smell to the design, layout, and colours, so much about that shop felt familiar, but then I noticed something a bit unusual. In the corner of the store, speaking with a lady, stood a dreadlocked man wearing what looked like an oversized crocus bag that fell to his bare feet. In his hand was a wooden staff and at his side was a bag that revealed the imprint of a Bible. As I continued to browse the store, our eyes met on several occasions, and each time, he would place the palm of his right hand to his chest and gently dip his chin, with a graceful and reassuring smile. There was some kind of energetic dance of eyes and body language happening between us, and I anticipated that there would be a conversation. But never would I have imagined that minutes later, I would disappear with him through the hills of Cape Town to spend three days at a Rasta camp.

His name was Naphtali, and he was a member of the Twelve Tribes Rastafarian sect. I can't imagine what our initial conversation entailed to make me think that disappearing for three days with an absolute stranger was a good idea. However, what I do remember is calling my mother from a payphone to tell her I was going to a Rasta camp in the mountains for a few days with a guy I had just met. As expected, her response was something like, "You're going to do what?"

To which I hurriedly replied, "Yup, it's safe, trust me. Love you, Mom. Byeeeee."

As we left the city streets and walked the dry hilly terrain, Naphtali caught me off-guard by losing his crocus-bag covering to indulge in a naked waterfall shower, or what at home we would call a spring bath. We walked for another hour or two and acknowledged that even though we weren't sure what had happened in that store, it felt like we had known each other for some time. Naphtali shared that he had noticed the Ethiopian Orthodox cross around my neck, picked up on my Caribbean accent, observed my movements, and knew he had found a brother.

That afternoon we arrived at a nearby village, where he introduced me to his family, friends, and other members of his community. I stayed with Naphtali and seven of his "brothers", who called one another by their tribal names. According to the month of your birth, you were considered to come from a particular tribe. I was born in January and so was also from the tribe of Naphtali. Among the eight of us, there were also three who went by the name Gad and two from the tribe of Judah. Strangely, though, it always seemed that when someone spoke and called a tribal name, you knew exactly who they were speaking to.

We shared openly and spoke about God, Christ, humanity, apartheid, politics, and what it means to be Rasta. They shared the struggles of identifying as Rasta in South Africa, and I shared stories and tales of Trinidad.

One of the things that struck me most about my time with Naphtali and his brothers was their sense of gratitude for everything. We took the time to acknowledge every flower, fed every stray animal, and greeted every individual with a momentary gaze, usually followed by a hug. There was never a moment or a conversation when I felt someone wasn't interested, listening, or seen.

The room we slept in was bare, except for a couple of mattresses, an old couch, and a few sheets of foam rubber on the floor. Images of Haile Selassie, Jesus, and the Lion of Judah decorated the walls among red, yellow, and green banners. Eight of us stayed in this one room, and even though there were several windows and a door, none of them was ever closed. Every morning, with the first beam of light, whoever opened their eyes first would proclaim, "Give thanks for life! Jah!" This exclamation would then be followed by a resounding chorus from everyone in the room: "Rastafari!" To this day, there are many mornings when I open my eyes and can still hear the resonance of their voices in my head. Their lives were simple, and they lived in full appreciation of all that life had to offer. Whatever little they had would be enough.

We prayed together every morning, every night, before every meal, and every time they prepared to take a sacramental smoke. They grew *Cannabis sativa* and the smoking of it for them was a religious sacrament and was only done in ritual. There was never the continuous or casual rolling of joints, setting of bongs, or smoking. It was not a social act, an escape, or a habit. They would only smoke twice a day, at specific times, seated together in a circle, and the ritual always began and ended with prayer. Even those who chose not to smoke – myself and two others – were still required to take part in the ceremony.

I recall one night they took me to what in Trinidad we would call a "Rasta dance". In other words, this was a community party with blaring reggae music, but their version of it didn't serve alcohol; heaps of marijuana lined the room. While other individuals were smoking casually, for Naphtali and his brothers, smoking was not taken lightly and was not about getting high, not even in a social setting.

We were all on the dance floor enjoying the music and skanking. Then, casually, one by one, Naphtali and his brothers all began to sit in the middle of the dance floor. As they closed in to make a circle, brother Gad pulled me to sit at his side. With the music still blaring and the party jamming, among shuffling feet and swaying hips, we sat on the floor and held hands. We prayed, blessed the space, consecrated the smoke, and packed a chillum pipe. That pipe went around the circle twice before they offered a closing prayer. Then, with a resounding exclamation of praise to Jah, we stood and rejoined the festivities. Everyone else around us seemed unfazed by the occurrence and simply respected the space we had created. It was clear that Naphtali and his brothers had a reputation and were respected. Their lives revolved around intention, they saw everything as sacred, and expressed their appreciation for life in every way they knew.

Twenty years later, I wish there was a way I could express my appreciation to Naphtali and his family, but unfortunately, we were unable to stay in touch. I have tried to find them on Facebook and even asked friends from South Africa if they had ever heard of Marcus Garvey Township. My efforts have been fruitless, so for now, I show my appreciation with this story, these memories, and my commitment to live every day with intimacy and gratitude for the simplest of things.

Embodying Gratitude

As we expand our understanding of life beyond the obsession with comfort, pleasure, and security, we begin to view our hardships and struggles through a different lens. It is not that we dismiss or become immune to the pain and struggle, but rather than be overcome and paralysed by it, we realize these experiences offer opportunities for growth and development. This perspective increases our potential for gratitude, but it is also essential to look at how we embody that gratitude. It's easy to say that we are grateful, even that we are thankful for life's challenges and obstacles, but how do we show our appreciation?

While my intention is by no means to measure one expression of gratitude against another, some expressions of gratitude have become relatively superficial and habitual. It is not that we lack gratitude, but maybe we could bring more awareness to how we express it. For example, imagine someone brought you all the ingredients you needed to bake a cake, and you politely said, "Thank you," and left all those ingredients on the counter. You were indeed polite, probably grateful, and you expressed your gratitude, but there was no action that carried the depth of your appreciation. It was an automatic social response.

> The most valuable gift we have to offer anyone, or anything, starts with our attention.

On the other hand, if you had said "Thank you," taken those ingredients, attempted to bake a cake, or even asked someone else to do it, that would have brought more meaning to your gratitude. Even if that cake was a disaster and ended in a volcanic eruption of icing with a plastic spoon melted into your baking dish, you took the time and made an effort to show your appreciation.

Both intention and action are essential if we want to embody the depth of our gratitude; otherwise, our gratitude becomes automatic, mechanical, and superficial. Of course, not every situation will call for us to bake a cake or offer something physical as an expression of gratitude. The most valuable gift we have to offer anyone, or anything, starts with our attention, and that attention can be directed in various ways. When it comes to our relationships, it means creating the time and space to be with someone intimately. Of course, intimacy is often associated with love-making and physical affection, but I am referring to an intimacy that can also be shared with absolute strangers in passing moments. It might be looking someone in the eyes and pausing for a moment when you say, "Thank you." It could be a two-handed embrace when you hug someone rather than a bump of the shoulders, or listening and creating a safe space for someone to be heard and seen. This intimacy often requires us to be vulnerable, and includes not only the readiness to expose yourself and show someone who you are, but also making space for them to do the same. Exchanges that represent bonds of trust and security are some of the most significant displays of gratitude.

In a world where we seldom find the time to communicate our appreciation, it is essential to acknowledge that being appreciated reminds someone that the space they occupy makes a difference in the world. It empowers them, leaves them feeling valued, and gives them a sense of belonging. Showing our appreciation and embodying gratitude is one of the simplest and most powerful ways we can serve one another.

With regard to the human experience and life in general, consider that our appreciation lives in our commitment to grow and our efforts to make something of it all. In other words, rather than simply allowing life to happen and pass us by, embodying our gratitude would mean intentionally trying to use whatever opportunities we have to learn and positively influence the world. When challenges and struggles arise, instead of mindlessly saying things like, "Everything happens for a reason," our gratitude takes the time to explore those experiences and discover the growth and transformation that lives in them. This requires our attention.

All this said, while we may be overflowing with gratitude, we are often so guarded or rushing off to the next thing that we merely flirt with gratitude. Regardless of what the object of our appreciation might be or how we choose to display it, for gratitude to land, it must be executed not only with intention, but also attention.

A Roof over Your Head

Let's take a moment to imagine our world without the shade of trees, the warmth of the sun, and the majestic salty underworld of the oceans that make up seventy per cent of our planet. How about shooting stars, rainbows, the buzz of a hummingbird's wings, or the moon's crystal-like glow on a two-hundred-year-old tree? The sand between your toes, snow-capped mountain peaks, food on your plate, or the intricate intelligence of life that connects the smallest insect to the largest mammal? How about gravitational forces and planetary alignments?

It would be wrong to make mention of gratitude and not draw attention to the living, breathing entity we call Planet Earth. Our unconscious sense of entitlement runs so deep that we often don't even acknowledge the natural world or the solar system we belong to as something to be grateful for. As a species, we collectively cut down ancient forests, destroy ecosystems, exploit natural resources for personal gain, and disregard our impact on the planet to facilitate our conveniences.

This may be a massive generalization, and you may be filled with gratitude for our planet and all that surrounds it, but, again, it is essential to look at how we express that gratitude. Many of us are grateful for our planet and acknowledge what an essential role it plays in our existence, but then we come up with all these excuses as to why we aren't personally responsible. We often conveniently view the issue of addressing environmental sustainability as beyond the capability of any one individual.

In reality, not everyone has the knowledge or the opportunities to be an environmental activist, and maybe environmentally conscious choices aren't always financially possible. But more often than not, rather than give up any of our conveniences or modify our lifestyles, we simply surrender the issue to corporate legislation, political interest, and environmental organizations. It's easier to believe that our actions will not make a difference because there are billions of other people on the planet who aren't doing their part. Fortunately, this isn't about them embodying their gratitude: it's about you embodying yours.

As with all displays of gratitude, there is a difference between saying you are grateful and intentionally embodying your appreciation. The eco-warrior image has become hip, cool, and fashionable; this is a good thing, and I'm not bashing it. Even if some of us are only looking the part and could be doing more, the mere fact that it is finding its way to the forefront of social consciousness is reassuring. However, posting images of scenic landscapes and sharing eco-conscious posts on our social media feeds is not enough. If we are truly grateful, we would make whatever little changes we can to lessen our environmental impact, beginning with changes to our lifestyle. Sure, these changes may not always be convenient, but gratitude is always willing to overcome inconveniences.

Some individuals would view our relationship with the natural world as somewhat one-dimensional in that there is no direct and ongoing communication. It's understandable; for generations we have collectively distanced ourselves from nature, spent less time with her, seldom spoken with her, and even stopped listening. To some, the idea of speaking and listening to nature may even seem crazy or eccentric. We imagine that our natural world does not have the intelligence to communicate, appreciate, or feel. Too often we consider humans separate from and superior to nature; this anthropocentricity is problematic. Anthropocentricity suggests that human life has intrinsic value, while other entities (including animals, plants, minerals, and so on) are just resources to be exploited for the benefit of humankind. Ask yourself if this is honestly how you feel; if not, it may be time to develop a new relationship with the natural world.

If we are authentic in our gratitude and appreciation for this mother we call Earth, creating the time and space to be with her is essential. It calls for the same intention and attention we would give to any other relationship. Sit in nature, talk to her, stop and appreciate the sun on your face, let loose and stick your tongue out! Make the time to immerse yourself in any aspect of the natural world. Put your phone down, forget the social media post, and simply listen. Be still and remember who she is; let her know she is seen. This is what gratitude feels like.

Beyond Judgement

It would be difficult for judgement and gratitude to coexist. At the beginning of this chapter, we acknowledged that even our struggles and hardships have their purpose. While you may nod your head in agreement, and this might appear obvious on the surface, we often continue to judge things in our life as "bad". If we ever want a chance at experiencing the full circle of gratitude, we must explore and soften our judgement of the world and everyone in it.

> While a situation may be painful, if we can make space to acknowledge and appreciate the growth and transformation it might offer in the future, we can still cultivate gratitude towards it.

As long as you judge something as bad, you prevent yourself from seeing anything to be grateful for in that experience. While this may sound like a privileged view, labelling something bad differs from labelling it uncomfortable, challenging, or even painful. To judge an experience bad is essentially to wish it had never occurred in the first place and therefore erases all possibility of growth. While a situation may be painful, if we can make space to acknowledge and appreciate the growth and transformation it might offer in the future, we can still cultivate gratitude towards it.

When we are absorbed in the "judging mind" and label some aspects of our life as bad, this is all we will see. Gratitude, on the other hand, understands the human experience as an ongoing process that is balanced and continuously unfolding. Its perspective is more extensive than our individual experience or lifetime. It allows us to remain open to discovering the possibility of gratitude even in uncomfortable and painful situations.

This dynamic of judgement and gratitude also applies to our personal relationships. If we continually judge someone for their opinions and actions, it limits our capacity to be genuinely grateful for them and what they offer. On this note, it's essential to consider that, in many ways, the judgement we direct at others often stems from our judgements of ourselves.

On the one hand, a part of us knows we are capable of shaping a perfect world beyond our imagination. On the other hand, we find ourselves caught up in this human experience and sometimes feel that we just can't get it right. We constantly judge ourselves because we think we should have known better and done better. This attitude then translates into our relationships because we expect everyone else to know better as well. Rather than being grateful for what the individuals in our life bring to the table and the efforts they continue to make, we find ourselves constantly judging everyone else and often making the people in our lives feel that nothing they do is good enough.

It would be helpful to remind ourselves daily that we do not have it all figured out; as long as we're in human form, the chances are we'll never have it figured out. We are not meant to. Mistakes, growth, and learning are essential parts of the human experience. A crucial aspect of increasing our capacity for gratitude is cutting ourselves some slack and extending that privilege to everyone else.

To embody your appreciation for life's experiences, you must move beyond any judgement of them. Your gratitude for life is expressed by your ability to learn and grow from your experiences. It is embodied by your commitment to take accountability for your mistakes and your attention to doing better. No aspect of life is separate from another, and you cannot just embody authentic gratitude for any one part of the human experience, you must embody gratitude for all of it. Rather than being linear, short-sighted, and conditional, your gratitude comes full circle.

THE FULL CIRCLE OF GRATITUDE

Chapter 11: Questions for You

◇ What are some things you are grateful for in your life, and how do you embody your gratitude for them?

◇ Can you identify some uncomfortable and painful experiences that brought you growth and transformation? How did you feel while navigating the experience?

◇ How do you show appreciation for our planet and environment? Is it something you've considered?

◇ Are there things and people you are grateful for but might not have shown your appreciation? How can you change that?

◇ Can you recall times when your judgement of people or situations inhibited your gratitude for them?

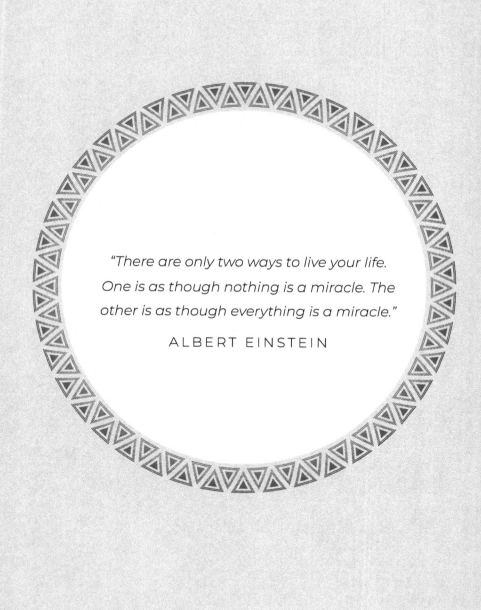

"There are only two ways to live your life. One is as though nothing is a miracle. The other is as though everything is a miracle."

ALBERT EINSTEIN

Resolutions of a Miracle Worker

We are no strangers to resolutions, so let's start there. Most familiar to us might be New Year's resolutions, but we also make birthday resolutions, weekly resolutions, and even daily resolutions. A resolution is a firm decision to do or not to do something. Some resolutions are more conscious and intentional, while others are subtle and somewhat automatic decisions. With regard to making significant lifestyle changes, resolutions are generally more intentional and revolve around health, nutrition, work, social habits, and our relationships. You have probably already discovered that resolutions don't always stick the first time around; sometimes they never do, and that's ok. However, what I want you to consider is not the lack of commitment toward your resolutions, but the nature of them.

For most of us, our more significant and intentional resolutions generally represent the change we want to see in ourselves, our lives, and our experience of the world. In other words, they often revolve around individual needs, wants, and desires. While it's powerful to identify where you can improve your life and your experience of it, there is a disconnect that arises when we get consumed with materialistic, surface resolutions in the process. These surface resolutions may improve our individual health, security, image, financial situation, and even our state of mind, but they do not necessarily create long-lasting evolutionary and conscious shifts.

Twenty-Four Hours Left

While a part of me would delight in pointing out all the surface pleasures, surface resolutions, and surface achievements that plague our society, it would be wrong of me to do that. I cannot define what "surface intentions and resolutions" means to anyone else, because we all have different priorities, intentions, and agendas. What one individual considers only of surface value could be filled with purpose to someone else.

Surface living is an essential part of the human experience and necessary in many ways. However, sometimes we get so self-absorbed and consumed by life's checklist that we treat the superficial things we consider "surface" as if they are priorities. Let's take a journey confronting your mortality to shed some light on what surface living may mean to you.

Imagine you have twenty-four hours left to live. You know that cliché, "Live every day as if it were your last." Well, it's here. Your time, the most valuable currency of all, has run out. I can't say what will come up when you're confronted with your mortality and given one more day to live, but I do imagine you might contemplate the impact you've had on the world. I wouldn't be surprised if you realized everything that once brought satisfaction and security didn't actually amount to that much.

I'm pretty sure your bucket list would disappear, and you would see life's checklist as nothing more than a social instrument that measured your success against everyone else's. Faced with your last moments, I would expect that you might see life through a new lens of appreciation, become more attentive, and begin to reflect on life beneath the surface. What hearts have you touched and inspired? Have you left any relationships unhealed? Who have you hurt? Could you have been more compassionate or loving? What contribution did we make to the lives of those around us?

Would meeting your mortality dissolve your narratives and judgements of others and allow you to see that everyone is navigating life with their unique challenges and conditioning? I'm sure there would be things you want to say to the people you love and those you may have mistreated, judged, and wronged. Possibly there was even someone you longed to love but never had the courage to. In these last twenty-four hours, you would probably wish you could rewind time and spend some of it differently.

But it's not over, you're not bankrupt yet.

What I'm getting at here is this: if you would *not* spend your last day on earth doing it or saying it, then it is possibly what I have been referring to as surface things. Personally, if I had one more day to live, I wouldn't go to my favourite restaurant, travel to an exotic location, buy new clothes, fulfil carnal desires, go to the gym, or buy a lotto ticket. I wouldn't spend my time trying to change someone's opinion, go shopping, or post pictures of my last sunset. Before throwing a tantrum here, I never said that surface matters were bad.

I would love to see a world with healthier people exercising regularly, being financially successful, and manifesting their dreams. Imagine a world where you can work less, do more things that inspire you, you are thriving, healthy, and have made an incredible life for yourself. Most of all, you are happy. Go wild here, dream big. These are all the things I wish for everyone.

But then what?

Yes, you heard correctly: "But then what?"

We have already acknowledged that you will leave your body one day, and so much of what you cherished as part of your human identity and experience will disappear, never to be spoken of again. However, as we previously noted, there are aspects of our lives, resolutions, and relationships that will live on long after we leave our bodies. In chapter 4, we saw how the vibrations of love and fear influence our world and shift the energy around us. We have all felt the emotions someone is experiencing simply in how they move around a room, their tone, their body language, or whether they look you in the eyes and how. We feel one another's emotions and impact people's energy in everything we do.

The law of conservation of energy we mentioned in chapter 4 implies that energy cannot be created or destroyed, but only changes state. In other words, I am implying that the ways you shift energy and the resonance of your life, choices, and relationships will live forever. This not only applies to the vibration and energy of our intimate relationships with family and friends but the store clerk, co-workers, passersby, the homeless, the abandoned, the selfish, the misguided, the sick, the wicked, the wronged, and even the wrongdoers. Do you get the idea? You are constantly in a relationship with everything around you, and all your relationships leave a residual vibration in the world – no exceptions.

The idea that our lives have the potential to shape our world and contribute to collective healing and evolution beyond our physical lifetime makes my heart sing. This realization invites us to consider the vibration and resonance of our choices and resolutions. It just might bring new meaning to the idea of living every day as if it were your last.

Is This Not Enough?

I lay outstretched and could still feel the sun's warmth radiating at my back. Even though the night sky moved in quickly, and the crescent-shaped moon hung low, the sand still emitted heat. Scattered clouds were making way for the stars to show off, the ocean lapped my feet, and there was a subtle dance of blue phosphorescence across the bay. Forty feet from my head, giant tropical trees swayed, creating a natural white noise that filled the gaps between nocturnal forest calls and rolling stones at the water's edge. There was no sign of humanity other than my body lying motionless on the sand, no lights, no voices, no screens, no engines, no hum of electricity.

Trinidad was five months into our third nationwide lockdown, and everyone was emotionally exhausted. Life was nothing like it had been pre-pandemic, and it appeared the rest of the world was returning to some resemblance of life as usual. Our schools had been closed for eighteen months, our government had declared a state of emergency, and there was no social life outside of breaking curfew or having sleepover parties. While the middle-to-upper class of Trinidad was still somewhat comfortable, the lower-income communities were out of work and struggled to make ends meet. The already enormous wealth and education gap between Trinidad's haves and have-nots was growing by the day, vaccine rollout was slow, vaccine hesitancy was high, and the division between the vaxxed and unvaxxed was worrying. It had been a long road, and there was no end in sight for our tiny developing nation.

Despite all that, I was lying on a beach in absolute serenity, under the night sky, at the edge of a virgin forest, with the ocean lapping my feet. Even though my circumstances were somewhat dreamy, my heart was overwhelmed with emotion, and I was consumed with what I perceived as loneliness. Blinded to the fortune of my circumstances, I spoke out loud into the wind and called out to God. I pleaded with him for clarity and insight. I asked that he guide my choices and decisions. I prayed for the courage to navigate the current state of our world with resilience, compassion, and love. In a moment of despair, I surrendered my life to God, to something greater than myself. That's when I had the nerve to ask for a sign.

I lay there and asked for reassurance that I was not alone, that I was part of something miraculous and divine, and that this was not all just an evolutionary accident. Imagine, that night, surrounded by enchanting and spell-binding wonder, I had the audacity to ask for a sign.

I got one. His voice was clear and firm but carried the comfort of a mother's first whisper to her newborn child. With a chuckle of disbelief at my ignorance, he asked, "Is this not enough?"

I was embarrassed that I would even ask such a question. I paused to digest the response and then couldn't help but smile to myself and whisper, "How much more proof do I need?"

The Search for Miracles

It's ironic that we are constantly searching for "the miraculous", because it's everywhere; we are surrounded by it. A miracle is something you can't explain with science or logic and only as the work of a divine intelligence.

While I understand it may be difficult for some of us to attribute our lives to a divine agency, I'm pretty sure we can all agree that life is full of many unanswered questions. Furthermore, even those questions that logic or science seem to have been able to answer or explain are not necessarily understood. One can always ask how or why. The reality is that every attempt to explain our existence brings a plethora of new questions and uncertainties. The search for the underlying truth of our existence can be summarized in three words: "We don't know."

When our understanding of miracles and magic is limited to all things supernatural and otherworldly, we overlook the miracles at our fingertips that are part of every living moment. We get so caught up in the routine of our lives that everyday miracles become ordinary and mundane. Our entire existence and all that surrounds the human experience is an unexplainable whirlwind of miracles. Contemplate the solar system, planetary alignments, photosynthesis, gravity, your beating heart, and the intelligence that guides everything in our world to function as it does. It would be absurd not to consider your very existence a miracle. Then on top of that, while I understand this *miracle world* might be a lot for some to accept, consider that you are not only part of an ongoing miracle but also an active co-creator within it.

To put it plainly, you can work miracles and, in many ways, are already doing so. Before you slam this book shut and shout, "Blasphemy!" – wait. Let's look at a definition of magic often attributed to American author Marion Zimmer Bradley. It is one that has always resonated with me and suggests that: "Magic is the shifting of energy at will." The idea of being able to shift energy at will only appears unrealistic because we have accepted a narrative of our world that is ordinary, and our role in it as chance. We have never been told of our full potential and have accepted things as they are, rather than understanding our ability to influence them. Meanwhile, there is a magic wand in our hand, and we are waving it around as if we were trying to catch flies with a toothpick.

This reflection is not about questioning science, religion, or our day-to-day logic. The intention here is simply to assist us in recognizing that magic is not some far-off, supernatural phenomenon, and that miracles are not acts reserved for a select, gifted few. You are part of a team of miracle workers that makes everything come together to shape our reality. You may not consider yourself a wizard or sorceress, but we continually participate in magic; we just need to become more aware of how we work our magic. It is in your body language, your smile, your touch, your words, your thoughts, your choices, and your resolutions. When you acknowledge that you are a miracle worker, even in the smallest ways, it comes with the responsibility to look at how you work your magic.

The thing about magic is that it's not always used in an uplifting and positive way. Magic can have unfavourable impacts if used unconsciously, and is even sometimes used with ill intentions. While there are times when we intentionally direct our attention and energy in a positive way, it's essential to look at the times when we unconsciously misuse our magic. There are times when we might be triggered, short-tempered, self-centred, frustrated, or simply disconnected from the effects of our actions. Remember that we are constantly shifting energy, and more often than we would like to believe, our actions and choices may be having a negative impact. No miracle-worker wants to acknowledge they contribute to shifting energy in a way that causes harm or misalignment, but an essential aspect of learning to be intentional with our magic is taking accountability for our misuse of it.

Dungeons & Dragons

I vividly remember the day I was told I was responsible for all the dreadful things happening in the world: judgement, separation, suffering, war, environmental disaster, oppression, corruption, mistreatment of animals, abuse . . . the list goes on. I sat there in disbelief, outraged, and ready to rise to my defence. How was that even possible? How could someone dare accuse me of such things after all that I had been trying to do to make the world better? My accuser was someone I considered my mentor, teacher, and friend, and I was heartbroken.

At that time, I was aware that my thoughts, actions, and words had the power to influence people, shift the energy in a room, and in many ways change the world. It was a concept that had empowered and inspired me; but there was something I was missing. I was so busy looking into the light that I had failed to acknowledge the darkness – my darkness.

I believed in a connectivity that made up the fabric of our existence and understood that each of us contributed to the evolution of humanity by elevating our consciousness. In other words, I understood that if every individual could embody more compassion, understanding, and love, their actions would encourage others to do the same. I imagined that our actions, thoughts, and words function like cosmic algorithms within the consciousness network that weaves all creation together.

> Your words, actions, and thoughts are equivalent to likes, clicks, and shares. The more you embody kindness, compassion, forgiveness, and fearless love, the more you contribute to these things going viral among humanity.

What in the world is a cosmic algorithm? Take, for example, the way social media algorithms shape the world of social media: the more likes and clicks a post gets will lead to more visibility, which leads to even more shares, likes, and clicks. The cycle continues until that post has gone viral and has in some way infiltrated every aspect of our digital world. Well, this cosmic algorithm operates in much the same way. Your words, actions, and thoughts are equivalent to likes, clicks, and shares. The more you embody kindness, compassion, forgiveness, and fearless love, the more you contribute to these things going viral among humanity.

Unfortunately, I was conveniently missing that the same cosmic algorithm also applies to the fear, judgement, oppression, greed, self-centredness, and the sense of otherness we allow to fill our lives. When we take part in these misalignments (even unconsciously), they go viral as well and contribute to the world's suffering and disconnect.

That day, as I sat with these accusations, heartbroken, with my emotions welling up inside, it all became apparent. While I was genuine in my efforts to embody the understanding, forgiveness, and love that I wanted to see more of in our world, I was also unconsciously contributing to the pain, the suffering, the oppression, the ignorance, and the disconnect. There were relationships I had not healed, people I had not forgiven, and apologies I had not offered. There were narratives, biases, and opinions I was unconsciously feeding, and I accepted the misalignments among my social circles as normal. I contributed to the disconnect in our world by shutting down and becoming closed off to opposing perspectives and opinions. I encouraged overconsumption every time I purchased something I didn't need. I contributed to our world's lack of love and compassion whenever I turned away from someone in need and saw them as separate.

No matter how beautiful your intentions are, if you are not aware of how you are shifting energy, you could very well end up practising magic that sows division, disconnect, and suffering. Your potential to work miracles comes with a responsibility to become present and mindful of how you use your magic. Focusing solely on your contributions to the light, love, and all the good you do in the world would be one-sided. That's the fairy dust and broomsticks of magic. As a miracle worker, you must remain committed to making your unconscious actions conscious. You must acknowledge and be accountable for how you contribute to the very aspects of our society that you consider out of alignment, the dark aspects of our humanness that you wish to dissolve. After all, the only way to illuminate darkness is by having the courage to walk into the depths of that darkness and turn the lights on. These are the dungeons and dragons of magic. Your working of miracles will never be complete unless you venture into your dungeons and confront your dragons.

Entry-level Miracles

Awakening to your potential as a miracle worker gives new weight to the choices and the resolutions you make. As with any other skill or art, the more you put it into practice and intentionally engage with your magic, the stronger it becomes. If we live without intention, we may one day find that we have been waving our magic wand around aimlessly and using our magic to manifest surface desires, blow stuff up, or put the fizz back into soda pop. I can't imagine this being a responsible use of our magic, and don't think Gandalf the Grey, sitting on the sidelines, would be too impressed.

The entry-level stages of being a miracle worker call for us to become aware of how we shift energy and to be more intentional with our resolutions. Environmentalist Jane Goodall said that rather than ask ourselves if we can change the world, we should bring awareness to our current impact and ask, "What kind of difference do we make?" Every genuine miracle worker is in some way committed to serving others, healing humanity, and the evolution of our collective consciousness. That healing, however, isn't going to come from surface resolutions.

By all means, create the amazing life you have always dreamed of and fill that life with surface pleasures, lightness, joy, and laughter – but as a miracle worker, this should not be your primary agenda.

We can buy all the crystals and sage we like or participate in shamanic rituals, but without doing the work in our lives, it's only pretend magic.

Your magic should be directed towards healing your relationships, nurturing the world around you, accepting accountability where you need to, and embodying more of the qualities you would like to go viral. Being a miracle worker means walking into our dungeon and coming face to face with our dragons. It also means understanding that not everyone is prepared to do that just yet.

I understand this can all sound intimidating, but if we cannot intentionally shift the energy in our lives and relationships, it may prove difficult to consciously shift the energy of our world. We can buy all the crystals and sage we like or participate in shamanic rituals, but without doing the work in our lives, it's only pretend magic.

The journey of a miracle worker requires a commitment to something greater than the desires of our individual identity and calls for us to make the resolutions in our life that will live forever in the hearts of every living being. The hearts you have touched; the burdens you have lightened; the relationships you have healed; the battles you have fought in the name of compassion, righteousness, and love: these are the resolutions of miracle workers, and their resonance will never die. There is a crystal ball in your pocket, a magic wand in your hand, and fairy dust upon your lips. Now all you need to do is open your heart and get your head in the game.

RESOLUTIONS OF A MIRACLE WORKER

Chapter 12: Questions for You

◇ Can you identify some of the surface resolutions that bring necessary value and happiness to your life?

◇ Do you obsess over or prioritize any surface resolutions that could possibly have a negative impact on others or even yourself?

◇ What are some of the simple everyday miracles that you often overlook?

◇ If you could change the world with the wave of your wand, how would you? What could you commit to doing more (or less) of in your daily life to facilitate that shift?

◇ What resonance or impact would you like to leave behind after you leave your body? How would you like to have impacted the world?

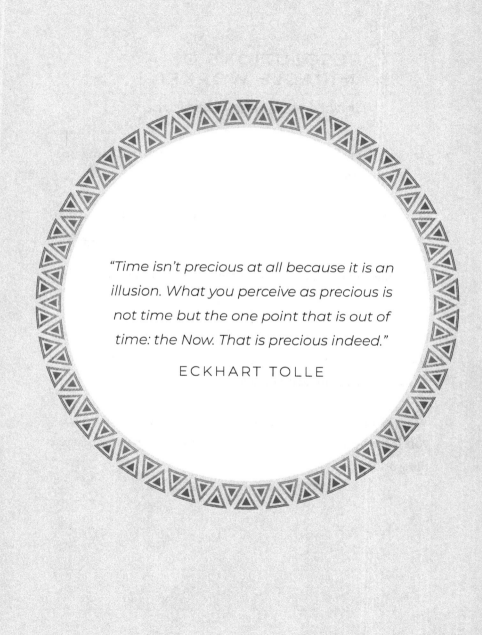

"*Time isn't precious at all because it is an illusion. What you perceive as precious is not time but the one point that is out of time: the Now. That is precious indeed.*"

ECKHART TOLLE

Timeless Medicine

This chapter is not about psychedelic plants, mushrooms, pharmaceuticals, or any other substances commonly referred to as medicine. It is not about anything you ingest, rituals you do on a full moon, or spiritual gurus who promise realization.

The concept of "living in the present moment" has been popularized by new-age spirituality and has become something of a cliché, but it has been medicine for generations. You don't have to be a divinely inspired spiritual practitioner to acknowledge that obsession with past or future events causes regret, anxiety, fear, and disconnect on many levels. We can find people from all walks of life echoing things like, "Be present! Don't live in the past! Don't worry about the future!"

The truth is that embodying the practice of being present as part of our lives is not as straightforward or as simple as it might appear. If we don't take the time to understand where the obsession with past and future events comes from and how it influences our lives, we will always be yo-yoing between the past and the future. More importantly, if we can't acknowledge that being present is multilayered and intricate, we could find ourselves in an unconscious bubble of avoidance while carrying unhealed emotional baggage around like a timebomb.

The medicine referred to in this chapter can dissolve our anxiety and worry, remove the veil of separateness, and remind us of what it means to love one another. It is a medicine that lives within us and is a timeless state of being that brings us to realize we are far more connected than we have been led to believe.

Puppet of the Past

I wish this were as easy as telling you that what happened in the past is gone and that you should just forget about it and move on. Poof! That's it!

Unfortunately, as lovely as it sounds, that would be absolute garbage. The reality is that the past impacts who we are and is continuously influencing our lives and how we show up in the present moment. There is no magic wand that can erase the memory and emotions of our experiences. Whether you consider your past experiences good or bad, they have an undeniable and ongoing influence on who you are. When we fail to acknowledge the impact of our past and how that shapes us, it gives the past power over our present experiences; it impacts how we navigate our relationships and show up in the world.

With regard to unpleasant and painful past experiences, if the trauma and impact of these experiences remain unconscious, or if the emotional wounds they left are not healed, they will likely contribute not only to your own suffering, but the suffering of others. The influence of these experiences leaves emotional scars and patterns that can sabotage our relationships and significantly impact our lives.

Pleasant and favourable experiences can also have a negative impact on our perspectives and relationships. While these experiences may have positively influenced us in one regard, if we aren't aware of the privileges those experiences have allowed us, they can limit our ability to empathize with others who didn't have those experiences. These favourable experiences can inspire you or give you a sense of confidence and security, but without a relationship to them, they also impart naivety and disconnect, and blind us to our privilege.

> We may not have the power to change the past, but we can change how the past influences our present state of being.

Regardless of the form our past experiences take and the degree to which they influence us, it is impossible to erase them, and any effort to do so can potentially lead to avoidance and denial.

Also, note that because you're not consciously overcome by regret or pain from your past does not mean the past has no hold on you. Our experiences, both big and small, cause us to develop unconscious habitual patterns and characteristics that begin to define how we behave. Naturally, if we are to process and heal from the trauma of our experiences or harness the growth they offer, we must acknowledge they exist and cultivate a relationship with them. Otherwise we become a puppet of our past. We may not have the power to change the past, but we can change how the past influences our present state of being.

Our Relationship to Change

Imagine moulding and creating a comfortable, secure, beautiful, and happy life that never changed. Wouldn't that be convenient? Everything would stay the same and be entirely predictable. Ten years from now, you would still have the same secure job and be doing the same things with the same people, and, to some extent, having the same conversations. Essentially you as an individual would be the same, and your life would become one predictable routine of happiness.

It may sound exciting at first, because you'd have a sense of security, and there won't be any unexpected challenges that threaten your sanity, but it also means that there would be no growth or transformation. No matter who you are or how happy you are with your life, you will eventually be bored out of your wits, become stagnant, and lose your passion for life.

Fortunately, you don't have a choice in the matter. Nothing will ever remain the same, no matter how hard you try, and change is not bad. It is not change that causes our suffering, but our relationship to it. The fact that all things are constantly changing makes life worth living and reminds us that every moment is uniquely invaluable. Imagine that there will never be another moment like the one you are experiencing right now. No sunset is the same, no kiss, no conversation, no individual. Even if you were to re-read these words one day, your experience of them would be different. Consider that an individual who lives until eighty would have breathed roughly 672,768,000 breaths in their lifetime, and not one of them would have been the same. In the words of the Greek philosopher Heraclitus, "No man can ever step into the same river twice, for it is not the same river, and he is not the same man."

When our identity or happiness is defined in any way by the circumstances of our life, it feeds our attachment to things as they are and creates a breeding ground for anxiety and worry. This can manifest in various ways – I'll leave the detailed introspection to you – but let's consider two general scenarios to gain some perspective.

Firstly, imagine that your life has aligned and you are surrounded by people you love, your career is all you could have imagined, you are financially stable, and all aspects of your life are remarkable. You are fulfilled, inspired, and happy.

Life, however, is doing its own thing: the river is moving, and a curveball (or two) is coming your way. Unexpectedly, you must move to another country or you'll lose your job; your spouse confesses to having an affair; and you have unexpected health complications to overcome. Change is happening, whether you like it or not, and while everything is going to be okay, right now you feel that your identity and security are being threatened. You are thrown into the unknown, and your life becomes a blur of fear and anxiety, which drives you to cling to anything that brings you a sense of comfort and security.

The flip side of this scenario also begins with your attachment, but the difference is that nothing appears to be going your way, and every day feels like a snowball of negativity and emotion. You find yourself overcome by the struggles of your everyday experiences and allow yourself to believe they will never change. In this case, you again identify with your circumstances and allow them to define who you are, but this time your perspective is layered with negativity. You find yourself thinking and saying things like, "I am sad. I am not good enough. My life is not going anywhere. I will never be happy again."

While these experiences and emotions are very real at the moment, it is essential to understand that they do not define you, and these circumstances will change. However, we must create the space for that change to happen. If we cling to present experiences and conditions, fearing things will only get worse, not only will we shut down any possibility of their getting better, but we will be continuously projecting that vibration of fear onto our lives.

As creatures who find comfort in security and routine, we commonly resist anything that threatens the alignment of our life as it is. That said, while we cannot stop the river of life from flowing, we influence its course through our responses and reactions. Even though momentarily uncomfortable, the unknown holds immense possibility, but we must allow the space for it all to unfold. That journey into and through the unknown could very well take us to a destination far more enchanting than anything we imagined.

The irony here is that your present experience of life very quickly becomes the past, and while you cannot influence the past, it continues to shape who you are in the present. If we do not maintain a relationship with our past experiences, we will find ourselves emotionally and energetically stuck. However, the only place we can be in relationship to the past is in the present moment.

Potential Rebirth

It might sound crazy and far-out, but, being made of divine stardust threaded together by one miracle after another and moulded in the image and likeness of gods and goddesses, we know we are always capable of being better versions of ourselves. You can put it however you like, but there is an intelligence within you that knows the potential of your greatness. However, an essential part of the human experience includes allowing ourselves space to make mistakes and acknowledge our humanness.

We have all done and said things we are not proud of, and we will probably continue to do so, more often than we would like to believe. Making mistakes is an integral part of the human journey and essential to our learning. The thing is, if we allow ourselves to be overcome by the guilt and shame of our mistakes, then we get stuck in the past, and it doesn't benefit anyone. If we have the presence of mind to acknowledge our mistakes and see how we could have done better, it creates a space where we can consciously choose to use those experiences and shape a new, improved version of ourselves.

This is a possibility that reveals itself with every breath we take. In other words, imagine that every breath offers us an opportunity to be reborn and become a better version of ourselves than we were before. At any point in time, you can choose to surrender the things in your life that no longer serve you, learn from your mistakes, and commit to being and doing better.

This might look different for everyone, but your rebirth doesn't happen next year, next week, or when everything conveniently falls into place. It happens now.

Equally important to note is that this potential for rebirth isn't exclusive to you. You must also extend this opportunity of rebirth to everyone else in your life as well, and this is where it gets interesting. It means allowing everyone else the space to be better, rather than defining them by their mistakes. No exceptions. The idea of forgiving specific individuals in our lives for the things they have done often comes with a "but". We can forgive, "but" . . . There's always that exception, that one person or thing that's unforgivable. Sometimes we say that we have forgiven someone, but we've never attempted to have a conversation with them regarding the pain. Then there are other times when the pain of an experience is so deep and hurtful that we find ourselves trying to erase any memory of it. Forgiveness is a personal journey, and every situation carries its unique weight that we as individuals move through in our own time. However, attempting to erase an experience and forget it ever took place is not forgiveness, it is avoidance.

I understand not everyone will be ready to heal and open to forgiveness; everyone will come to reconciliation in their own time. But we must do whatever we can to be ready when that time comes. Before we create a list of exemptions where forgiveness is not necessary or acceptable, note that forgiveness does not imply justification or acceptance, nor does it suggest that an act or deed should go unpunished.

To live in the present moment without interference from our past

> True forgiveness creates the space for someone to be better even when they can't see why they need to be better, or how.

experiences and trauma, or even that of previous generations, we must be open to genuine forgiveness. This forgiveness does not forget, does not seek validation, and is not dependent on an apology. True forgiveness creates the space for someone to be better even when they can't see why they need to be better, or how. Until we open the door to healing all our relationships, we will never truly understand what it means to be present. The past will always have a hold over us, and the pain it carries will always be in the background, navigating our lives. This kind of healing could take lifetimes, and while it may sometimes feel impossible, it is happening collectively in microscopic doses.

To give this some perspective, it helps to remember that the human experience is not about you, your healing, transformation, and realization. As we mentioned in chapter 2, the idea of "you" as separate from everything else is an illusion. You are part of a collective body of consciousness. There will be times when you are in alignment, ready to do the work, and actively contributing towards that healing, but there are other times when you are tired, overwhelmed, and struggling to find a way through. During these times, other individuals continue to do their work and pull their weight when we aren't able to. We are part of a team, and we all have a role to play, but that role may look a little different from time to time. When we cannot overcome the heaviness of our emotions, be sure that healing is still happening, but sometimes we are the ones being healed.

The opportunity to be reborn is something that extends to all human beings. To judge and define others by their past mistakes and actions is to keep them imprisoned in the past and rob them of the God-given opportunity to grow and to do better.

While this is not a chapter on forgiveness, it is crucial to understand all the aspects of what it means to *be present*. To be free of the past comes not only in releasing our attachments to what might have been; it is also in healing our guilt, shame, and pain.

Future Fever

Throughout this book, we have referenced the near-obsession with our security and all that surrounds the needs and desires of our personal identity. Another way this obsession influences our lives is through our constant cycle of planning, anticipation, and overthinking to ensure the future is favourable and all is taken care of. You might even think this is human nature and part of our survival instinct, and you would be correct. But in many cases, it is the very obsession with our survival that denies us the experience of being present. Furthermore, while it may be basic human nature to prioritize our survival, I can't help but feel that it is also our divine nature to evolve beyond the desires of self-preservation. Consider a spiritual evolution that magnifies our capacity to love one another, expands our sense of identity, and expands our understanding of the human experience beyond our physical bodies.

It is empowering and comforting to acknowledge that we directly influence our lives through our choices and that every decision we make contributes to shaping the future. However, no matter how much you think, worry, anticipate, or fantasize about what is to come, the only time and place you can influence your future is in the present moment. This gives our choices more weight and makes it even more critical that we are present and paying attention when making those decisions.

To give this some context, imagine that your life is a masterpiece and you are an artist. While your imagination is artistry and you are filled with inspiration, you cannot create a masterpiece simply by dreaming about it. You must feel your feet on the ground and be in the moment when everything else disappears so that you can transfer that inspiration to the canvas, one intimate stroke of your brush at a time. While an artist steps to a canvas with a vision, their vision remains fluid and can change at any point. At completion, that masterpiece may not even resemble what was envisioned when it began, but something far more exquisite.

Your life is a living, moving, breathing masterpiece. Every choice and action is a stroke of your brush, and you must be conscious and aware of what you are creating at every moment, much like an artist would be. Not only will your opinions, views, and understanding of the world continually change, but so will your inspirations, desires, needs, and intentions. In crafting the masterpiece of our lives, we must remain present to all that is changing.

There is nothing wrong with envisioning our future to manifest the lives we desire, but when we get attached to these stories and visions, we find ourselves blinded by expectations and anticipation. This, as you would imagine, breeds anxiety and disappointment when things don't exactly play out as we planned. Regardless of your commitment to manifest the reality you dreamt, things will usually look a little different. Sometimes your life will bear no resemblance to anything you imagined, and other times you might realize that the life you created is the one you dreamed of when you were twelve, but not the one you desire today.

Along the way there are moments when the universe screams at you to change course, life slaps you in the face, and everything urges you to stop and pay attention. Unfortunately, we remain so committed to the previous vision we had for our life that we ignore all the signs and push through the anxiety to force a dream of our past; a dream that no longer serves who we are in the present and a dream that no longer exists.

There are universal powers at play that dream far greater dreams than we do, but we must be present and listening if we want to give that dream a chance.

Dreams of Pelé

Throughout my life, there have been many times when I thought I knew exactly who I was, had a clear vision of what my future would hold, and was willing to do whatever it took to make it happen. As you might imagine, it didn't always go as planned, and my earliest memory of a dream-shattering, life-altering, identity-stripping experience was at fourteen years old.

I lay in my bed with a football clenched to my chest and tears gathering at the corners of my eyes. My body shook as I came face to face with defeat. Hugging a second football between my legs like a pillow and feeling the warmth of a third resting at my back, I remembered my soccer coach and mentor telling me that I should "Sleep football." To my young and eager imagination, that translated as "sleep with my footballs". While I understood that wasn't what he meant, I was determined to go the extra mile and do whatever it took. I slept with three to five footballs on my bed every night, until that night. Looking back on it now, I can't help but wonder how my mother entertained such a thing, because there was never really any football-washing ritual before bed. It wasn't uncommon for me to have blades of grass and clumps of dirt under the sheets when the morning came.

I studied videos of the legendary footballer Pelé, I woke up at four in the morning to train in my backyard before school, and I dreamed of being a professional footballer. I would never miss a day of training and knew that commitment and dedication were my only ticket. I wasn't the fastest or the most talented, but I knew the game and wanted it more than anything. When not on the field, I studied strategy, practised technique, and longed to understand all aspects of the game. At football camps, I never won the trophies for the most valuable player or goals scored; I was the kid winning awards for "Most Dedicated" and "Most Improved", and I didn't win too many of those, either. Hard work and humility were my only chances, because the truth is that I was surrounded by far better players, and I knew it.

Over the years, my commitment and dedication paid off, and I had become a solid player – with my heart set on becoming one of the world's best. At fourteen, I envisioned football scholarships and was plotting the next step when I got an opportunity to attend a football camp in Leicester, England – the kind of camp that attracted football scouts and youth clubs to check out the upcoming talent. It would be the first time I had travelled outside the Caribbean to play football, and I was in for an awakening.

That camp shattered my dreams of becoming an international football star. Not only did the sixteen-hour daily training regime take a toll emotionally and physically, but the level of skill and ability I encountered was far beyond anything I had imagined. There were kids half my age with more talent, vision, and ball control than players I revered on Trinidad's national team. I was in absolute awe of what these kids could do; their knowledge of the game; and their ability to put the ball anywhere they wanted at any point in time. On top of it all, their commitment and dedication made me feel as if my football dream was merely a part-time hobby. I was way out of my league and confronted with a life-altering realization.

It wasn't even a week after returning home that I told my coach that I was going to take a break from football; a break I knew would last a very long time. He believed in me and gave me so much of his time and energy that I couldn't help but feel that I would be a disappointment if he knew I was walking away. That night I lay in my bed, and with heart-wrenching despair, I surrendered my dreams of being a professional footballer. I couldn't imagine what my life would be like without football. It was all I did or ever wanted to do. While part of me wanted to push harder and practise more to manifest those dreams, the truth was that I knew without any doubt that there was something else in store.

> Resilience is essential to overcome the challenges and hurdles that arise, but if we aren't present to the signs and omens that appear along the way, that resilience becomes ignorance.

I'm sure we all have our own stories of navigating shattered childhood dreams, but it appears that as we grow older, we get stuck in the narratives of what our lives are supposed to look like. We become attached to these stories and end up swimming against the current, trying to force these versions of our lives. Resilience is essential to overcome the challenges and hurdles that arise, but if we aren't present to the signs and omens that appear along the way, that resilience becomes ignorance.

That night, lying in my bed, I closed my eyes and asked God to show me the signs, shape my life, and guide me. To this day, I have faith that I am still being led and guided to and through a version of this human experience that is greater than I could have ever dreamed.

The Human Projector

While I'm sure we can all identify ideas and visions for our lives that we are somewhat attached to, this isn't the only way we can be overcome with future fever. Sometimes we simply choose to write narratives about future experiences and then project these narratives onto future events with an imagination that rivals any nail-biting, heart-thumping TV series. We manifest the most dramatic, jaw-dropping, emotionally charged, and sometimes borderline delusional possibilities, then project them onto everything and everyone. Kind of like when your boss calls for an urgent meeting, and you think you will be fired because he's a vegetarian and you had a steak for dinner. How about that social media post your ex-boyfriend intentionally shared to remind you that you will grow old alone? Or the publisher who turned your book down, as a clear sign that you'll need to sell everything and move back in with your parents? Then there's that social event you have to attend, but you're convinced that you will be laughed at, ridiculed, and eventually hung from the ceiling like a piñata while the host streams it live on his social media feed. We all have our versions of these projections, and chances are you know what I'm talking about.

I'm sure you might see how projecting narratives like this onto our lives creates unnecessary anxiety and worry, but it's so much more than that. Remember that your mind shapes your reality, and your thoughts carry vibrations. While your host might not string you from the ceiling like a piñata, the mere entertainment of that thought impacts the energy you bring into the experience. If we unconsciously project negative thoughts and vibrations onto our lives, it will negatively impact those experiences. There are times when our intuition is warning us or preparing us for a challenging situation ahead; however, it doesn't serve anyone if we allow ourselves to get lost in fear-driven narratives and projection. The ability to remain present while creating the space to understand our fears and concerns, or dial in to the messages of our intuition, gives us the foresight and tools to positively impact what could be a negative experience.

On the other hand, our projections are not always negative and fear-driven. We also sometimes let our minds run away with excitement and eagerness. Maybe someone agrees to go on a first date, and you've already started envisioning your life with them, your family, and perhaps even written your wedding speech. I can't tell you the number of times I was sure I'd bought the winning lotto ticket and began to imagine my life living off the interest and using the rest of it to uplift humanity. I am pretty sure I even called my cousin to tell him the epic news.

I am not implying that the practices of conscious visualization, affirmations, and the power of manifestation in our lives do not exist. I am saying that they do, and they are powerful; this is why you must keep your head in the game. Not only must we remain present so that we can identify when we are feeding into an unrealistic emotional narrative, but it is essential that we consciously and intentionally reinforce our positive visualizations with actions, or very little will come of them.

Either way, whether we are projecting favourable fairytales or delusional dramas onto our lives, the power of the human projector is real. If we are not in a relationship with our projections, we will find ourselves filled with anxiety or overcome with disappointment.

The potential of the human projector calls us to be present so that we can consciously begin to shape our lives and reinforce our visions with action. Rather than wonder what a conversation will be like, we prepare ourselves to have it. Instead of anticipating the loss of a loved one, we take the time to love them, so they are never lost. Rather than dreaming of our success, we discover the success that comes with living intentionally in every moment; in that moment, we begin to glimpse life as it truly is.

The Search for Purpose

Purpose is what sets our hearts on fire, and without a sense of purpose, you could find your life becoming somewhat stagnant. You may have checked all the boxes, achieved a desirable level of success, maintained a comfortable lifestyle, and yet find that happiness still eludes you. A sense of purpose can give your life meaning and reassure you there's a reason for your existence and that you make a difference in the world.

Every individual connects to purpose in their unique way. Some of us relate purpose to our role in society, career, or even the manifestation of goals. Others may view purpose through a bigger lens and associate it with battling humanitarian issues or attaining spiritual realization. There is no limit to what your purpose might be, and throughout your life you will connect to your purpose in different ways. After all, everything is constantly changing, and you are part of that everything; so are your purpose and your relationship to it. The problem is that we often think of our purpose as one thing in particular, perhaps something we *will* achieve someday, a cause we have dedicated our lives to, or something we desire to become. Unfortunately, if this is the case, there is something that most of us are missing.

It was on the banks of the Ganges in India that I was reminded of what my purpose was. I was at an international yoga festival there and attended a workshop by Tommy Rosen. He is a recovering addict and has found his way to sobriety with the help of his yoga practice. At thirty-eight years old, I had pretty much been sober for my entire life and knew that no matter how much I thought I understood about the struggles of addiction, the reality was that I could never truly understand. There is no more extraordinary teacher than firsthand struggle, realization, and triumph. That day Tommy Rosen was my teacher, but not in the ways I had anticipated.

After grounding his participants with some breathwork and meditation, he posed a question to the group that could be considered somewhat generic: "Who knows what their purpose is?"

I chose to remain quiet as hands began to go up. A series of responses followed, some that resembled the ones that churned in my head, others that appeared to come from a far-off, flowery land.

"To learn to love."

"To remember God."

"To discover our truth."

"To work through our karma."

I wondered if people understood the meaning behind their words or just said what they felt Tommy wanted to hear. This must have gone on for about five minutes as I quietly listened and noted my internal reactions to every response. Then Tommy looked at us with absolute confidence and said: "Your purpose is to listen to me speak."

My internal dialogue went something like, "Huh? What the fuck? That's a little arrogant, Tommy. Who do you think you are?"

I can't recall much of what Tommy said immediately after that, because it took me a moment or two before I could get out of my head. Then I realized that he was not coming from a place of ego; it was a teaching that dissolved the influences of our ego. It was a "truth" that I often spoke about as being one of the initial pillars of yoga practice.

While listening to Tommy, I allowed the fluctuations of my mind to critique and analyse his statement. As long as I allowed that to happen, I could not be present to understand and absorb what he was saying. My chattering mind had created a narrative that pulled me away from my purpose at that moment: to listen and learn from

Tommy. It's like in our reflection on conversations from chapter 10, when we looked at the times we say we are listening wholeheartedly to someone, but in reality we are crafting our response in our heads. We are not present or listening at all.

In hindsight, our search for purpose often distracts us from experiencing what is happening right now. Our obsession, longing, and attachment to a life purpose can prevent us from discovering the meaning in every moment. When we fixate on the larger life purpose we dream up, we end up missing all the little moments of purpose that contribute to that dream in real time, the moments in which we have an opportunity to change lives every day. It's like playing a video game (some of you may remember Mario Brothers) where you are running a race and obsessed with getting to the finish line. You might miss all the opportunities to collect the tokens along the way, only to discover that the tokens you missed were worth more than crossing the finishing line. Or maybe those tokens led you through a sacred portal to another level, or where you conquered the entire game.

Your only purpose is to be present to life and all it brings: the ups, the downs, and the in-between. Like stepping stones, every moment presents a unique opportunity and experience that leads you to another moment with its unique purpose. Some moments may feel uncomfortable, others uplifting, and some may even be disguised as a complete waste of time. Regardless, finding our purpose in every moment will reveal the opportunities to begin weaving a web of collective purpose. Together we are here to fulfil one larger purpose, and there is an intelligence that understands the real purpose of our existence. Your primary individual purpose is to be present, listen, and feel, then let that intelligence teach you and guide you, one moment at a time.

Medicine

We get so consumed by spiritual practices that we mistake religion, gurus, rituals, psychoactive plants, and even lifestyles for "The Medicine". I have dedicated the last fifteen years of my life to the practice, study, and teaching of yoga. If I did not feel that the practice of yoga increased our capacity to love one another and deepened our relationship with God, I would walk away from it immediately; but yoga is not The Medicine. The Medicine has nothing to do with postures, sexy bodies, handstands, or traditional texts. Furthermore, The Medicine is not in ancient teachings, chanting, chakras, planetary alignments, your body's storage of DMT, coffee ceremonies, or your microbiome. If these things set your heart on fire and prepare you to receive The Medicine, then by all means. However, note that while all these things may have medicinal properties in and of themselves, they are not The Medicine.

> We get so consumed by spiritual practices that we mistake religion, gurus, rituals, psychoactive plants, and even lifestyles for "The Medicine".

I am not here to promote the practice of yoga, but I will reference the philosophy briefly to drive this point home. It is simply the language I am familiar with and rings true for me. Imagine you had no previous conceptions of the word yoga and that it is not a practice that has swept the world by storm.

Think of yoga as a state of being in union with all things. The state of yoga is one in which the ego dissolves, and there is no otherness or separation. In other words, it is the realization that you are part of one intricate and divinely inspired collective body. However, as long as the mind is fluctuating, it creates the concept of *you* and *me, we* and *them,* even *then* and *now.* The mind creates separation because it identifies with our individual identity and sees everything as *other*, which then births the need for self-preservation.

Only when we are in a conscious relationship to the mind and able to quiet its fluctuations can we be entirely present without narratives and projections; only then can we embody that state of union. At that moment, we see everything as an extension of ourselves and can begin to dissolve the illusions of the smaller self and acknowledge God in everything and everyone. Many practices like meditation and yoga offer us tools to increase our capacity to be present and help us dissolve the lens of duality and otherness. However, I must emphasize that these practices and philosophies are not The Medicine; these practices only prepare us to activate The Medicine that is already within us.

The Medicine, my friends, is the ability to be in the here and now without interference from past experiences or future considerations. To live our lives in intimacy with everything around us and acknowledge our connectivity to all of it. To be present and feel both the light and dark as aspects of ourselves. This is freedom from the fluctuations of the mind. This is freedom from time. In that moment of freedom, there is no *you* and *me*; there is no otherness, no competition, no judgement, no success, and no failure. There is no worry, anxiety, expectation, or disappointment. In this moment, outside of time, we become The Medicine.

It is here real love exists, and it is here that we begin to witness God.

TIMELESS MEDICINE

Chapter 13: Questions for You

- ◇ Are there any areas of your life where you are currently resisting change?

- ◇ Can you recall a major change that improved your life and created space for growth, even though it was uncomfortable at the time?

- ◇ Are there any past experiences that negatively impact how you show up currently in your life? How do they influence you?

- ◇ Have you ever projected negatively onto future experiences? Why do you think that happened? What were you most afraid of?

- ◇ Do you intentionally use projection or visualization in an effort to manifest things in your life? How do you back up your visualization with intentional action?

- ◇ Can you identify times when your mind took you away from your purpose of being present in the moment?

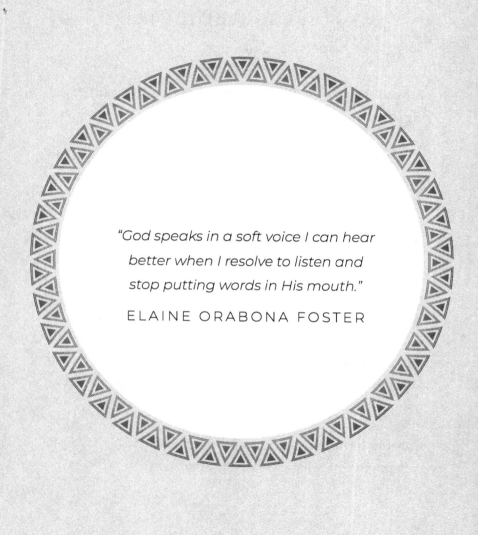

"God speaks in a soft voice I can hear better when I resolve to listen and stop putting words in His mouth."

ELAINE ORABONA FOSTER

Ears of the Heart

We have been told many stories of God, angels, and divine beings communicating with prophets and mortal men. It could be in the Bible, the Quran, the Bhagavad Gita, or texts of almost any spiritual tradition. There is almost always a tale of divine insight, revelation, or teaching shared with us humans.

We could probably debate whose story came first, how it should be interpreted, and which version of divinity holds more power and authority, for centuries to come. This reflection however, is not about who God spoke to, what God meant, or how God appeared. The issue in many of these tales is the underlying, subtle, and limiting portrayal that God *spoke* – past tense. Furthermore, that "He" only spoke to a select few chosen and gifted individuals.

I can't help but wonder how different our world would be if, as children, we were told that God speaks directly to all of us, and were taught to listen for his insight and guidance. This idea will seem radical and even blasphemous to some people, while others may have been encouraged to have a direct relationship with God. Ironically, our relationship and communication with God are often only validated as long as they reinforce previous teachings and accepted practices. Otherwise, it is often implied that we are delusional or have been misguided.

Some of us have never attempted to nurture a direct relationship with God because we've been too busy listening to everyone else – to social voices that tell us who God is, what God said, and even what God wants of us. We have been told by everyone else but God.

Whatever your idea and concept of God may look like, divinity has always spoken directly to you. God has never stopped whispering to your heart. Every one of us. We have plain and simply stopped listening. We have been distracted and overcome by all these external voices that tell us what to do, say, and think. Then we become consumed by the voices within our heads trying to get clarity amid all these opinions and noise. Our minds have become so loud with all these voices trying to be heard that we can no longer identify the voice of God.

But rest assured, God speaks to you. If you can quiet your mind, you will find God's whisper resonating within your heart.

The Ego of a Grape

Let's imagine that we had an orange as a friend. Yes, Mr. Orange had all the required social skills and fitted perfectly into your life. The only problem was that he thought he was a grape. Mr. Orange truly believed he was a grape. The thing is, if Mr. Orange ever wanted a chance to discover he was really an orange, he would first have to realize that he was not a grape.

You are probably wondering where I'm going with this and

thinking the example is ridiculous. Tuning into divine insights is undoubtedly far more complex, right? Well, not necessarily. What I am getting at here is that to hear God's delicate divine whisper in your heart, you must be able to identify the voices that scream over it. Much like Mr. Orange, who must know the difference between an orange and a grape to realize that he is not a grape, we must know the difference between the voices of the mind and divine insights from God so that we can distinguish between the two.

Throughout this book, we visited various aspects of our identity, which is precisely where the voices of the mind begin. As we have noted before, our personal identity is partially tied to everything, from our name and image, opinions, beliefs, careers, and even lifestyle. These characteristics are not only things that other people identify us with, but things that we ourselves identify with. All these aspects of our identity have a voice and influence the version of ourselves we present to the world. They are the voices of your mind, and they seek justification, validation, security, acceptance, and satisfaction, and feel they have something to prove. These voices of the ego have strong opinions, and if we do not have a relationship with them, every choice, decision, and possible moment of clarity and peace will be interrupted by the constant chatter of the mind.

I wish I could tell you that the voices of the mind sound like X, while the voice of the heart sounds like Y, but it's just not that simple. On the one hand, the voices of the mind are conditioned by our past experiences and social influences, constantly worrying about what people will think, what everyone might say, and how they will react. On the other hand, these voices can also be selfish and sometimes serve our personal needs and desires above everything, regardless of what others think. In other words, we do and say whatever brings us immediate satisfaction, regardless of our impact on the world around us or the people in our lives. In this case, while the voices of the mind may not have been worrying, over-analysing, or overthinking, there was no conscious presence or awareness. In other words, there was no heart.

As if navigating our internal voices wasn't enough, we also have each other's voices to navigate. That's right. We project our ego-driven voices onto one another through our perspectives and opinions. We live in a world of screaming and shouting egos. We tell others how they should act or feel based on our interpretation of their identity, who we think they are, or who we want them to be. Our families, our friends, and our social media feeds all give us their opinions in an attempt to influence our actions. Then we have community leaders, teachers, gurus, music, and books (even this book). These are all external voices of influence. They are just as loud as the ones inside your head and feed much of our constant internal chatter. However, these external sources have no clue how you genuinely feel regarding any situation or what your heart is guiding you to do. And even if you told them, they wouldn't necessarily understand.

While external voices can help make sense of what you are feeling, the only way you can truly feel at peace with any insight or way forward is when it resonates with the knowledge of the heart. Your authentic voice lives within your heart. This voice of the heart is still. It is a voice that does not think; it knows. It is not a voice that we hear, but feel. The voice of the heart is not concerned with the past or the future, and it lives in the timeless medicine we discovered in the previous chapter. While the heart's voice is not as loud and boisterous as the voices of the mind, it is direct, clear, and consequential. When it comes to the voice of the heart, there is no questioning or worrying about reactions, approval, or the thousands of possible outcomes that await you. The heart is not concerned with any of that.

It's important, though, to note that the voices of the mind are not useless and offer us valuable insights and opportunities for reflection.

I recall hearing the lyrics, "Today is a good day for my ego to die." They are words sung by an extraordinary musician and songwriter named Nahko, and they landed in an interesting way for me. While I related to the desire to kill my ego, the introspection that followed made me realize that killing my sense of self and identity would diminish the human experience and treat it as worthless. I began to understand that the ego has its place. I decided it would be far more powerful to hold my ego's hand and mould a loving relationship filled with possibility rather than kill one of the greatest teachers I ever had.

The Heart Knows

The wisdom of the heart should not be confused with the logic or overthinking of the mind. The voice of the heart reveals an absolute sense of knowing that becomes clear when the mind is quiet. It is the heart that holds a receiver tuned to the frequencies of God. The heart I am speaking of is not your physical heart but the core of your being; it is the thread of divine intelligence woven into every timeless moment of your existence. The heart knows precisely where we are meant to be and what we need to experience. Sometimes, the heart is fully aware that it's leading us onto a battlefield and knows we are in for an uncomfortable or borderline excruciating experience, but the heart does not make mistakes. You may be wondering how the heart can be so sure. Well, consider there is only one intelligence of the heart that whispers to all of creation.

Imagine that the voice of the mind is ego-driven and belongs to the individual,

> The voice of the heart reveals an absolute sense of knowing that becomes clear when the mind is quiet. It is the heart that holds a receiver tuned to the frequencies of God.

whereas the heart's intelligence is collective and in alignment with everything. The voice that guides my heart is the same voice that guides yours. Sometimes it guides us differently, even in opposite directions, or puts us on what appear to be different teams, but its intention is to bring all things into divine alignment. It understands that each of us needs specific experiences to fulfil our curriculum; its agenda is our collective growth and realization.

When we ignore the voice of our heart, we can feel the misalignment in our lives. Nothing seems to go smoothly, and everything appears to have hit some kind of speed bump. We may lack motivation, inspiration, and find it hard to connect to the joys of living like we used to. It's almost as if our lives become burdened with a subtle and invisible weight. Even though we push through and pretend that everything is okay, or fill our lives with surface pleasures and distractions, the voice of the heart continues to whisper, and we know something needs to shift.

Creating the space and finding the courage to make that shift isn't always easy. The mind's voice always comes up with "what ifs", "buts" and any excuse that convinces us to remain in our comfort zones of security, avoidance, and routine. The shift the heart is calling for could revolve around a relationship, a job, a conversation, a lifestyle, a habit, or even an aspect of our life that we consider insignificant. The moment we decide to listen to our heart and take the leap, everything begins to move. This shift may even bring uncomfortable conversations, cause emotional turbulence, and sometimes disappoint the people we love, but discomfort and challenges have always been part of the journey. Whether we are on our knees or have brought someone else to their knees, the heart knows it is necessary at times.

When we acknowledge and listen to the heart, it sends off a resonance that touches all aspects of our lives and everyone in it. That resonance sounds something like a divine command from the universe to all that surrounds you: "Troy's ready. Let's move! Autobots, transform and roll out!"

As it all begins to unfold, we find subtle shifts and decisions becoming magical opportunities, beautiful and profound individuals randomly make their way into our lives, and everything aligns in ways we could not have foreseen. We remember what it is like to be in alignment and filled with the joy of living. As motivational speaker and bestselling author Gabby Bernstein might say: you can feel that the universe has your back. Looking back, we can usually see exactly where that shift began: that one choice, that one decision, that moment when you placed the whisper of your heart above the loud echo of your mind. Whether you acknowledge it or not, that was the voice of God. This divine whisper of the heart is not concerned with your praise or whether you give it a name. It will guide you regardless. But it does long for you to listen.

Roots of the Mind

Naturally, the more we tame the egotistical voices of the mind, the less raucous they become. We are not shutting them out per se; we are simply not reacting to the mind's noise. It's as if we can acknowledge these voices and then create the space to check in with the heart's voice to see what that is saying. The mind and the heart are not enemies, nor are they always in opposition; they simply view the world a little differently. The mind responds to life with planning, logic, and calculations. The heart feels, listens, and aligns with an extensive intelligence that reason cannot always understand. The more we create the space to listen and amplify the voice of the heart, the more the mind softens its approach and can now acknowledge that there is another voice to be considered.

It is crucial for the heart and the mind to have a balanced and holistic relationship. The voice of the heart, while it is the ear to God's whisper, does not always trump the mind. The heart needs the logic and reasoning of the mind, or it can get carried away. When this relationship lacks balance and leans too heavily towards the heart, we get overwhelmed with emotions and obsessed with our ideas of the ideal world. We could find ourselves with our heads in the clouds and somewhat disconnected from the impact of our actions and what's happening on the ground. The mind's voice is like a workbook for the heart. Without it, the heart may get carried away, skip a few lessons, copy some answers, or even drop out of school thinking it's got it all figured out.

I have sometimes heard that we must elevate the heart above the mind, and while I can see the necessity of that in many situations, the mind and its reasoning are essential to living in this world. We must elevate the heart and ground the mind, but not necessarily place one above the other. Where these two meet and coexist in balance is where we discover our potential to embody genuine and authentic love, not just talk about it.

The intelligence of the heart connects you to God; this is where God speaks to you, guides you, and inspires you. The voices of the mind connect you to the world and give you a sense of individual identity. They are the roots that keep the heart grounded in the human experience so you can do your work in the world. The mind and heart need one another. The big picture is that God has work to do in this world and wants to use you to do it.

Divine Downloads

When a friend told me he had received a download, I wasn't exactly sure what to make of it. He had used the term to imply that he had an idea. While I had never before considered an idea as a download, it made me wonder where these ideas came from, and it made sense to refer to them as downloads.

However, I do not believe every idea qualifies as a download. The seed of an idea originates in the mind as a thought, an internal suggestion, or a question that calls for further investigation. However, a divine download is a bit different in that it hits you at the heart level and, as you might imagine, leaves no room for questioning or doubt. The clarity these downloads bring is undeniable, and when they land, you experience an instant moment of knowing.

The thing about these downloads is that they usually don't make sense to anyone else. Divine downloads can come in the form of inspiration, insight, a stroke of brilliance, or even a call to action. They can apply to a relationship, a creative idea, a new perspective, a business venture, or anything, really. I believe we have all experienced divine downloads, but we may not have recognized them as such.

Several years ago, I received some of these downloads that altered the course of my life in ways that I could never have predicted. After running my hemp store for seven years and struggling to navigate the challenges of the retail world, I began to consider my future and whether I was truly impacting the world in the ways I desired. The thought of giving up all that I had built and represented was heartbreaking, but it became clear that I needed to change the direction of my life. I wasn't sure what it would look like or how to make it happen, but I knew I didn't want to run a retail store for the next forty-plus years.

My heart had been heavy with this realization for a few weeks when I pulled into my driveway one afternoon and got out of my truck to the robust and enlightening whiff of diesel fumes. I describe those fumes as enlightening because they carried a significant download. I immediately knew I needed to set an example and make a statement regarding our environmental responsibility. With diesel fumes lingering in my nasal cavity, I thought to myself, "I'm going to show our third-world, short-sighted, fossil-fuel-drunk leadership that alternative fuels are a real possibility."

I had no clue what that example or statement would look like, but I did know that diesel vehicles could run on an alternative fuel called biodiesel, and sometimes even on vegetable oil. The thing about these downloads is, they don't reveal the big picture immediately: they only reveal one step at a time, and call you to act by giving you moments of inspiration. You can change course or revert to what is familiar and safe at any point along the way. However, if you have the courage and the faith to answer the call, you will continue to receive one download after another.

I answered the call two weeks later by flying to Colorado to learn how to make a biodiesel processor so that I could run my truck on alternative fuel. When I returned home to Trinidad, I realized that the biodiesel processor was a little too risky, as it involved methanol, and I was concerned that I might blow myself up in the process. However, the trip was in no way a failure, because I had gained a wealth of knowledge about alternative fuels and the waste cooking-oil industry. Instead of making biodiesel, I decided I was going to convert my truck to run on waste cooking oil. My mechanic thought it was hilarious, but entertained my request to instal the conversion, while my family wrote the venture off as a crazy environmental project. After months of collecting waste cooking oil to fuel my truck, I couldn't help but notice the obscene amount of waste oil dumped by restaurants into drains and waterways. This brought another download, and it would be big: I would close my hemp store and invest everything I had left in a business that would collect waste cooking oil. The business would be called Ecoimpact, and it was going to collect used cooking oil from restaurants, then clean and recycle it to be resold as biodiesel feedstock (a raw material used in producing biodiesel).

The voices of my mind, along with the external voices from my family and social circles, screamed, "Are you a fucking lunatic? You are throwing everything away to collect garbage? Who are you going to sell it to? Why would anyone buy it? Just join the family business already! No one cares about the environment here in Trinidad."

In a society and economy driven by subsidized fossil fuels, and a culture that places no value or emphasis on environmental sustainability, this move was bold, courageous, and borderline idiotic. Regardless, these downloads were clear, and every time I encountered an obstacle along the way, I was called to have faith. All the voices that criticized and doubted my choices were filled with fear: the fear of failure, the fear of loss, and the fear of the unknown. I feared I would never get the smell of old cooking oil off my skin. At that time, I didn't have a conscious relationship with love and fear, but fortunately, I knew how to follow my heart.

It was only a matter of weeks before I purchased a collection vehicle, hired my first employee, and found myself drenched in vegetable grease every afternoon. I took every cent I had, invested in equipment, set up a processing plant, and began reaching out to fast-food outlets across the country. The move was scary, challenging, and riddled with obstacles, but every step along the way, it felt right, at least to me. I recall the expression on my father's face when potential buyers flew in from North America and Europe to see the finished product and secure long-term contracts. It was a surreal mixture of pride, excitement, and utter disbelief.

There were many reasons I might have decided to ignore those downloads. My choices were not logical, the decision to put everything into this far-out idea was not safe, and I cannot recall anyone thinking it was a good idea. However, those divine downloads put my life on a very distinct path, shaped a successful waste-oil recycling business, and in many ways, crafted my life so that I could teach yoga, write this book, and now entertain a career in speaking.

I cannot say exactly where my life would be today if I had not dared to follow those downloads, but the more I reflect on the many decisions and strokes of inspiration throughout my life, I wonder, "What if I hadn't. . . ?" Divine downloads can be subtle and appear as ordinary ideas or random thoughts, but acknowledging that we receive inspiration and insight from divine sources is the first step to hearing them. These downloads will be clear, you will feel them in the depths of your heart, and they will call on you to act, often in defiance of the mind's logic.

Processing Software

While these divine downloads can come at any time, it should be no surprise that they usually arrive at moments when the mind is quiet. Remember, these downloads are not ordinary, passing thoughts of the mind. If the mind is overactive, it creates anxiety and dis-ease that inhibit our ability to process these downloads. In the same way computer viruses, increased web traffic, and dingy software interfere with our internet downloads, the fluctuations of the mind interfere with divine downloads.

In earlier chapters we looked at the importance of cultivating a holistic relationship with our mind and how daily practices of stillness and meditation enable us to quiet the mind. Of course, we also noted that the idea was to take that stillness into our lives and live with more intention. This means that there are many times when the mind can be still and present even though the physical body is in a state of action. These divine downloads do not only come when we are meditating or in prayer; they can arrive at any time as long as we are present, grounded, and in the moment. They can come during yoga practice, when we're driving, surfing, gardening, cooking, or even making love. These are the times when we are entirely absorbed in whatever we are doing at any moment. The more we cultivate a relationship with our mind and nurture our ability to be present and immersed in life, the clearer the channels for the heart to receive these divine downloads.

> Divine downloads are often beyond the mind's understanding and challenge our own expectations and plans for our lives; this is why they are sent directly to the heart – your heart.

When receiving these downloads, it is vital to note that no matter how much your heart is set on fire by them, the mind will question everything. That is its nature. Furthermore, the external voices of your life will not always understand or agree with these downloads. Your friends, family and social circles will probably think you've lost the plot. They will worry that you are illogical and irresponsible and they will try their best to impart reasoning. The thing is that if these downloads were meant for anyone else, they would have received them. Divine downloads are often beyond the mind's understanding and challenge our own expectations and plans for our lives; this is why they are sent directly to the heart – your heart: a message that no one else can hear or feel but you.

In processing divine downloads, be present to the software you choose to use. The software of the mind is inclined to ask the question, "If . . . ?" followed by "But . . ." Lots of buts. The software of the heart is more advanced and will ask the questions, "How?" "When?" "Where?"

When you become aware of these divine downloads and can

process them on a heart level, they keep coming, take on a new shape, and begin to influence all aspects of your life. Divine downloads are always cued and waiting. They are waiting for you to be clear-minded, still, and ready to act.

EARS OF THE HEART

Chapter 14: Questions for You

◇ What kind of things are the voices of your mind concerned with, mostly? What do the voices of the mind sound like, and how do they impact you?

◇ How do the voices of your friends, family, and social circles define you? Do you feel pressured to meet expectations, and how does that impact your choices?

◇ Recall a time when you felt something in your heart that you knew to be a clear call of inspiration that wasn't exactly logical? Did you have the courage to follow through, and can you identify a shift in your life if you did?

◇ Can you relate to the concept of divine downloads, and what gets in the way of you answering the call?

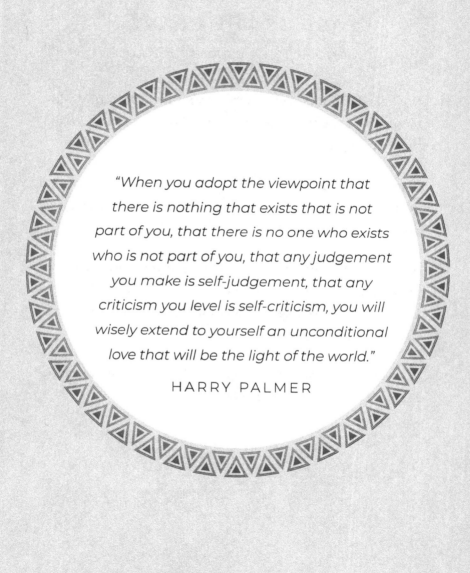

"When you adopt the viewpoint that there is nothing that exists that is not part of you, that there is no one who exists who is not part of you, that any judgement you make is self-judgement, that any criticism you level is self-criticism, you will wisely extend to yourself an unconditional love that will be the light of the world."

HARRY PALMER

The Wings of Love

Love can ignite fires of inspiration, dissolve identities and differences, bring the invincible to their knees, wage wars, and even bring those wars to a peaceful and swift end. Love builds bridges, but can also burn them down. Love can be the wind in our sails as we traverse universal oceans, or it can gracefully sink us and put us to rest with the Titanic. Love has no shape and no box can hold it. Love is infinite, untameable, and beyond definition.

I can't think of any other word more diverse in its use and powerful in capacity. Love can describe anything from our sentiments and emotions to a universal concept of harmony and everything in between. Love is mentioned more than three hundred times in this book alone, and we haven't even talked about chocolate, wine, or Indian food. It can be used to describe actions, intentions, sentiments, or even a state of being. Some might even use love to illustrate a divine agency and connect to statements like: "God is Love". While this is a beautiful sentiment that many can relate to, love and God

> To know and experience true love is the greatest of all privileges.

have more in common than we might realize in that they have both been misrepresented and misused for generations. Imagine that with all the possibilities of love, socially we usually see love portrayed in a way that limits our understanding of it to that of attraction, attachment, and pleasure.

You see, much as we said concerning God, because we have been told of love does not mean that we know love, especially when the version of love we have been fed by society is conditional and bound by expectations. While well-intentioned, this kind of love is a misguided and self-serving imposter.

To understand love, we must be willing to have an intimate, vulnerable, and possibly uncomfortable look at our relationships and the conditions we have placed on our love. To know and experience true love is the greatest of all privileges. The love discussed in this chapter is not abbreviated to "luv", attached to your food, or shot on arrowheads by Cupid. This love embraces all human experience and everything that surrounds it. This love is an intimacy of the spirit, our spirit.

Conditions of Love

As a kid, I was told that God loved us unconditionally and gave us absolute freedom to choose. I knew this was true, but I was also taught that God would banish me for eternity if I didn't choose right. Even at eight years old, I knew something about this rendition of freedom and love simply didn't add up. I understood without any doubt that love was unconditional, but this love appeared to have a fair number of conditions.

I am only offering this up for consideration because this concept of love has shaped an understanding of what love is for many of us. It has led us to believe that love is circumstantial and conditional. Of course, we say that our love is unconditional, but we unconsciously surround our love with the limits and boundaries that serve our agendas. It has bred a narcissistic and selfish understanding of love where we use the fear of punishment and emotional tactics to manipulate our loved ones. We have come to know a love that we reserve for those who love us in return. In many instances, if someone were to upset us, do us wrong, stand up in opposition to our opinions and beliefs, or begin to live their lives in a manner we disapprove of, we would withdraw our love. As long as the object of our love acts in accordance with our interests and well-being, then our love remains.

While it pains me to make the comparison, in many cases, love has almost taken the shape of a business deal and is loaded with the emotional corruption we looked at in chapter 9. "I will love you as long as you . . . " Then we turn the tables, and you get something like, "If you love me, you will make me happy, and . . ." Sure, we may not use these exact words, but if we take a moment to have an honest look at the energetic exchanges of our relationships, I'm pretty sure we can fill in some of those blanks. We use our love to disguise our threats and ultimatums. It is a concept that has infiltrated religion, parenting, intimate relationships, and our everyday relations. We must begin to recognize that *real* love has no conditions, limits, circumstances, and no ifs or buts. Real love is not limited or governed by the narratives, needs, and desires of your smaller identity.

What Love is Not

The potential of love is immeasurable, and the possibilities of love are infinite. While it may challenge our conditioning, consider that not only can love live anywhere, but that love lives everywhere. When we give love a definite shape and form, we find ourselves looking at situations and deciding whether love is present or not. We ask ourselves, "Is this love?" But love is always present. Our desire to understand love must guide us to explore: what (or who) is being loved? And why?

In many cases, the very situations we would label as being devoid of love are filled with love; it is just a love that is selfish and self-serving. This is not to completely disregard the importance of self-love, which has become somewhat of a modern-day craze. There are many ways in which we must love ourselves so we can remain centred and grounded to love others. However, while loving oneself sounds exciting, and you can find individuals from all walks of life screaming the call of self-love, it's important not to get carried away. The ego is so sneaky that it sometimes uses self-love to deny responsibility, avoid accountability, and disguise our dissociation from the world. If we lose touch with the more significant idea of extending our love beyond our limited personal identity, then our love only serves our comforts and desires. We become unconsciously driven by a love that revolves around self-gratification and self-preservation. Many of us would probably be tempted to deny that this is love at all, but it is love; it's just a love that is limited and self-centred.

Love is everywhere. It is the very essence of our existence. I understand that we might look at situations of greed, jealousy, oppression, dishonesty, and even inhumane acts and ask, "How can love possibly exist here?" However, consider that there is love in these situations, it's just the love of power, greed, money, ego, control, ideals, and ultimately a love that serves one's personal needs and desires. When we view these situations as being devoid of love, then love is dead; you cannot grow or mould something that does not exist. If we can identify that love does exist in these situations, but that it is a selfish and self-serving love, then we can work towards helping someone reshape their understanding of love, redirect it, and expand that love outwards.

Let's give this a little context within the realm of intimacy and romance. Firstly, let's acknowledge that love is not a romantic relationship, love is not sexual relations, and love is not marriage. Love can absolutely include all of these things. It can be the foundation of all our intimate relations. Love in and of itself is pure intimacy. However, just because there is romance, sex, or marriage, does not necessarily mean there is the understanding and embodiment of love in its fullness.

Romantic love is only one manifestation of love. A romantic relationship has a particular shape and structure with expectations that our society or belief systems adhere to. We can hope that love lives within and surrounds a romantic relationship, but romantic relationships do not define love. If a romantic relationship ends because circumstances change or expectations can no longer be met, love should continue to exist. If the love between two individuals ends when a romantic relationship dissolves, we must question whether the fullness of love was ever present or if it was merely a limited love unconsciously driven by security and personal desire.

When we authentically look at a relationship and ask, "What is being loved?" we might discover there is more love for the relationship itself and the security it provides than for our partner. We become so obsessed with the structure of a relationship and the comfort it offers that we use tools of intimidation and manipulation to hold the relationship together, even if it rips our partner apart.

Before you run away with a narrative here, I am not encouraging the abandonment of relationships when we have a hard time or when things get tough. Intimate and romantic relationships take work, and they can be some of our most outstanding teachers. We must be careful not to obsess and fall in love with an idea of a relationship or the security it provides us; that we don't prioritize those things over our partners. If we intend to dissolve the unconscious boundaries we place around our love, even within our romantic and intimate relations, it would serve us – once again – to ask, "What or who is being loved?" at any point in time.

While the infinite and enormous love we speak of can exist within our romantic and intimate relationships, it is not limited to these relationships. This love cannot be defined by structure, conditioning, or limits. It is not reserved for the select few who meet our expectations and respond to our desires with a smile. This is a love that is forever expanding and touches every corner of our planet, along with everything and everyone on it. There is nowhere that this love is not. This is a love that breaks the chains of social logic, dissolves the narratives of our individual identity, and flies free of limits and conditions. Your love is ready to fly.

Mosquito Martyr

One evening, I was at a birthday celebration chatting with a friend and we got into some rather powerful introspection. By no means was the environment conducive to such conversations, but regardless, it appeared that this one was destined to happen. Her name was Betty, and I honestly can't recall how the whole scenario played out, but one moment she was sitting across the table, and before I knew it, she was next to me, and it was as if we had been sucked into a vortex. We talked about her past relationships, therapy, trauma, pain, hurt, forgiveness, anger, resentment, and pretty much anything that came up. There was no hidden agenda here. She put all her cards on the table and was essentially saying, "Help me make sense of this." Given her sassy, sarcastic personality, it would probably sound more like, "Make some fucking sense of this – now!"

Betty was open about the experiences causing her pain, both past and present. While it was clear that she genuinely wanted to be free of her anger and resentment, she was consumed by the illusion of her identity – as we all often are. In other words, she was taking everything personally. The narrative Betty created had her believe that everything had been done and was being done directly to her, spitefully, with the intention of causing her pain. I offered a new perspective and tried my best to explain that everyone in her life was simply doing the best they could with what they knew. I explained that people sometimes don't know any better and find themselves repeating old patterns and reacting to situations in familiar but unhealthy ways. Betty always had a "but" no matter what I said, "But . . . but . . . but . . ." However, as she began to realise that I wasn't justifying any of the "wrongdoings" done to her and that she wasn't under attack, something shifted, and "but" slowly became "maybe".

In addition to understanding that we all have our own experiences and conditioning that shape who we are, I invited her to consider another possibility: the possibility that on a subconscious level, she may have chosen to help others grow by providing the opportunities and circumstances for them to do so. In doing this, however, sometimes it meant that she became a casualty. I was not invalidating Betty's hurt and pain, but offering a perspective that could help alleviate her anger and resentment. If we can relate to one another on a soul-to-soul level and see past our separate identities, we begin to see others beyond their conditioning. Acknowledging that someone's conditioning is not truly who they are makes reconciliation not only possible, but inevitable. If our personal identity consumes us when we experience sadness, hurt, and pain, we will often feel that it is a personal attack. However, on a soul level, these experiences simply become interactions in which we are helping one another work through our shit and find our way home. We are not only each other's teachers, facilitators and support staff, we are the curriculum.

I felt we were making headway and that Betty was at least considering a new perspective on her relationships that held possibility. That's when she slapped her arm violently and screamed, "You fucking mosquito! How dare you?" I looked down at her arm and saw a splotch of blood and the mangled legs of a mosquito. In a moment of clarity, I decided to seize the opportunity, and with a smile on my face, I held her arm and said, "Are you angry at the mosquito?"

She replied, "Of course I am! He fucking bit me. Look at the size of him. Look at my arm."

I asked if she felt the mosquito had intentionally bitten her.

"Yes," she replied, "He knew exactly what he was doing."

I explained that the mosquito was simply doing what it knew to do and that while he was consciously coming in "for the kill" to suck her blood, it wasn't personal. He was just doing what came naturally to him due to his conditioning and she happened to be the target.

Her smile said that she understood the point, and then she concluded with a bit of flair, "He chose to bite me because my blood is the sweetest."

That unconsciously heroic mosquito was a martyr that laid down its life as an instrument of reflection and teaching. Even if he was conscious of what he was doing, even aware that it would cause Betty some discomfort, and chose to do it anyway, there was no personal motivation behind his actions. He was simply doing what his insect intuition had shaped him to do.

Not Everyone Knows Better

It's easy to say that someone should know better and do better, but what if they were never shown how? Some of the most powerful privileges in our world are extremely subtle and not spoken of or considered often enough. They mould our characters, shape our perspectives, and make up the very bedrock of our conditioning.

Author and activist Maya Angelou once said, "Do the best you can until you know better. Then when you know better, do better." I believe that if someone knew better, had the tools to do better, and in any moment was truly able to, they would.

Before we dive into the subtle privilege of knowing better, I want to acknowledge the impact of our living conditions and other external stressors that sometimes inhibit us from doing better, even when we know better.

Imagine what it would be like to navigate life without access to electricity, clean water, or heating. How about giving up your vehicle, access to childcare services, or even your computer? Having to carry the ongoing stress of an autoimmune disease, crippling anxiety, or a life-threatening condition that could flare up at any moment? Then consider the experience of being a single parent, living with a physical disability, being stuck in an abusive relationship, having to work three jobs to meet your basic needs, or being consistently plagued with insomnia.

The list goes on, and on, and on. There are individuals among our society showing up every day and doing their best while navigating unimaginable conditions and immense emotional stress. Very often someone is walking a thin line between sanity and collapse when we point a finger and say things like, "Do better. Work harder. Why can't you smile? You're not living up to your potential. What's wrong with you?" In many cases, even when someone may want to do better and knows better, they simply can't, because their current situation or emotional baggage has hindered their ability to do so.

When it comes to someone knowing better, consider the most powerful privileges are those of love, safety, and security. The privilege of feeling safe; being supported by family and community; a community that encourages you to follow your dreams; people who believe in you, provide a sense of security, and will always be there if you need a lifeline; having someone to teach you right from wrong, guide you through the hows and whys of life, give you the freedom to make your own choices and mistakes, and love you unconditionally when you make those mistakes. To many of us, these things may be standard, but as sociologist Michael Kimmel notes, "Privilege is invisible to those who have it." To be raised or live in a reality that is devoid of these advantages has an immense impact on an individual and the emotional tools they have access to in navigating this world.

While this all may appear obvious on the surface, after years of contemplating the social disregard for the environment in Trinidad, I had a moment that allowed me to begin connecting some dots. It wasn't uncommon to see people randomly toss garbage out of their cars, throw it in the drain, or leave all their trash on beaches and riverbanks. I had a difficult time understanding the disregard toward the environment and our social acceptance of it. Then, one day, while outraged at someone casually tossing a KFC box out of their car window onto the lush-forested roadside, I was able to move past my disbelief and reflect on the experiences of that KFC-tossing culprit. I began to wonder how they could be so disconnected from the impact of their action and feel it was acceptable.

That's when I had an epiphany, and realized my own disconnect and ignorance. I had failed to acknowledge the reality that existed beyond my privilege. Many people were burdened with daily survival and trying to feed their families, pay bills, dodge bullets, and create anything resembling a favourable future. They lived on the poverty line in a developing Caribbean nation with growing inequality, where their basic need for comfort and security was not being met. Furthermore, they probably had never been taught the importance of the environment, how they impacted it, or even why they should care. Then, on top of it all, I expected them to be environmental stewards and make the sacrifices necessary to lessen their environmental impact for collective wellbeing – a collective in which they never felt included and wellbeing they had never experienced.

If an individual has never known what it means to be cared for or loved by someone, how could we expect them to care for others? An individual who sees their role models acting out, emotionally triggered, or abusive comes to understand those attitudes as their example of normal. This becomes their conditioning. If someone has never felt included, supported, or made to feel safe by a system or society, how can we expect them to care for anything beyond their own individual needs and desires? They live under the constant threat of survival.

It will always be easier to look at someone's life and form our opinions and judgements, but if we are not willing to understand their circumstances, experiences, and conditioning, we will only ever see them through the lens of our narrative. Of course this does not excuse any actions that are out of alignment, or punishment of them; but any genuine attempt to create real, lasting shifts within an individual must also make someone feel safe, understood, and loved. As suggested by an old spiritual teaching, "We have not come to teach, we have come to love, and love will teach us all."

Time to Fly

While this limitless and unconditional love may seem unthinkable and unrealistic, that's because the love we have come to know has been trying to fly without its wings. The teacher and philosopher Osho once said that love could not fly without the wings of freedom and forgiveness. I would like to expand on this analogy. Imagine that instead of having two wings, that love was a dragonfly, with four wings. On one side of the dragonfly's back sit the wings of freedom and forgiveness, as Osho implied, but on the other side sit the additional wings of compassion and empathy. Without any of these four wings, our love becomes situational, temporary, and limited by our expectations, narratives, and attachment to personal identity. In other words, we will find it difficult to embody the kind of love that soars.

The wings of empathy and compassion are somewhat easier to accept and understand than the wings of forgiveness and freedom, so let's begin there. Empathy and compassion allow us to transcend the boundaries of our individual experiences and relate to others as an extension of ourselves. Empathy gives us the opportunity to understand the experiences of others, along with the conditioning that shapes their opinions and perspectives. It is not only that we imagine what it might be like to be in someone else's shoes, but there are times when we share in the suffering, sadness, pain, and even their anger and ignorance. Furthermore, empathy also creates the space to consider the larger collective impact not just of our choices but also of social changes and global events. It's not always an exciting quality to have, and there will be times when considering the larger impact becomes inconvenient, and the burdens of others become too much for us to bear. Regardless, empathy is essential and opens the door to compassion.

Compassion in its truest form is love in action. Empathy doesn't exactly serve anyone unless we are inspired to act. Compassion acknowledges our connectivity to all things and is a commitment to serve others. It can be summarized in the age-old teaching, "Do unto others as you would have done unto you." We have been repeating it for generations, and while you would assume that everyone can relate to it, we often unconsciously place limits and boundaries on our compassion, much as we do with our love. We extend our compassion to our inner circles and our loved ones; then, outside of those circles, we feel that a situation isn't our problem or doesn't affect us. Sometimes we are so blinded by the narratives we've created that we fail to see someone's intentions and find it challenging to move beyond our judgement of them. There are even times when we consciously withdraw and withhold our compassion in an attempt to communicate disapproval or inflict some kind of punishment.

For those moments when your compassion feels like an inconvenience or that it hasn't been earned, I give you the words attributed to numerous spiritual teachers, "You cannot see God at all until you see God in all." Let these words echo in your heart, for if we see God in the eyes of every human being and the grace of every living creature, compassion becomes as natural as the air we breathe. Without compassion, we may understand the concept of love, but we will never know the embodiment of it.

With the wings of empathy and compassion, your love may have the confidence to fly, but with two wings on one side of your back, your dragonfly of love will only fly in circles. Freedom and forgiveness are the wings that expand our horizons and act as a compass so we can navigate our lives from a place of love rather than fear.

Freedom is essential for love to exist, to offer each other the freedom to choose our own path and make our own mistakes without the fear of judgement and condemnation. The intelligence of life itself includes the shifting dance of cause and effect that facilitates our growth and understanding, but it is not the role of love to govern that. Love is meant to support us through and in spite of our choices and mistakes, not govern us with threats in an effort to influence our actions. Without freedom, the fear of judgement and punishment guides our actions, and as long as we are guided by fear, those actions can never be born of love. Fear is a hindrance to love.

Imagine being in a relationship where your partner constantly did

> If your love is guided by the fear of judgement or punishment, then your love is motivated by self-preservation; the foundation of your love is self-serving.

things that set your heart on fire and made you smile. Then you discover that they do these things not because they love you, but because they are afraid of how you'd react if they didn't. This, of course, does not mean they don't love you, but it means that those actions were driven by the fear of your reaction. Wouldn't it have more of an impact on you if they acted purely out of love?

Let's take this up a notch. Consider the divine agency of your understanding. You can call it whatever you like, but we have made it this far, so let's call it God. Imagine that we did everything we could to live our lives with utmost love and compassion for everyone, just as God wanted. Would it be more pleasing to God that we acted out of the fear of punishment or because we saw the hand of divinity in all of his creation and could not contain our devotion?

If your love is guided by the fear of judgement or punishment, then your love is motivated by self-preservation; the foundation of your love is self-serving. If we wish our relationships to be a catalyst for a love that is infinite and all-inclusive, then we must allow one another the freedom to choose our paths without fear of condemnation. Without that freedom, our relationships will be compromised by an air of ownership and manipulation. Furthermore, our love will always be restricted to one that serves our personal needs and desires.

It shouldn't take us too long to connect the dots here. Freedom cannot exist without the wing of forgiveness, and for many of us, it is the most troublesome wing of all. We have already established that we are all human and make mistakes. Sometimes we unconsciously make choices that hurt others, and there are also times when we are aware that our choices cause others unimaginable pain, suffering, and heartache. Whether within our relationships or our society, there will always be unacceptable acts deemed inappropriate, out of alignment, or that threaten the well-being of others. I will say again that I am not suggesting we forget and ignore wrongful deeds, nor that these acts go without being addressed. Our response to these acts may resemble punishment and must communicate that these acts will not be condoned. However, we should always have rehabilitation and reconciliation as our end goal rather than retribution. We must do everything we can to build bridges instead of walls and create space for understanding, resolution, and forgiveness. In some cases, this may take time, even generations, but we cannot walk the path of love if we do not open the door of forgiveness.

Very often we find ourselves justifying the exceptions, limits, and conditions that we place on our love and deciding who is worthy of it or not. Regardless of how impossible it may appear at times, our love cannot fly to infinite heights without the four wings of empathy, compassion, freedom, and forgiveness. If we are to embody this love, we must understand that we cannot truly love anyone unless we love everyone: no exceptions. However, while the invitation to extend this love, with all its four wings, to everyone in your life might bring forth a series of anomalies or doubts, it's essential to remember that love comes in many forms. Love is not always pleasant and uplifting. It does not always tell us what we want to hear, or fulfil our wants and desires. Love can be challenging, fierce, courageous, in your face, and sometimes even momentarily hurtful, but above all, it always flies with its four wings.

What Does it Mean to Love?

The concept of love, as I have come to know and understand it, is the very core of the human experience. There are many ideologies and perspectives that attempt to explain why we are in human form and give some kind of meaning to it all. Some of these narratives and beliefs are supported by ancient manuscripts that have survived the test of time, others appear to have been crafted by delusional and brilliant minds, and some have been shaped to manipulate and influence the masses. The truth, however, as with many things, is that we just don't know. With that said, it only makes sense to me that we have embodied human form to remember and re-learn what it means to love one another beyond our individual needs and desires. Every chapter of this book, in some way, is intended to facilitate our journey to embodying that love.

This journey includes many obstacles, challenges, illusions, and distractions that we must overcome. However, none of them is as misleading and influential as the identification with our physical bodies and our limited identities. It probably began centuries ago with the evolution of our egos, which manifested narratives of separation, otherness, ownership, and competition. Then, as if these narratives were not crazy enough, in many ways some of us began to project them onto our understanding of God, giving divinity egotistic qualities; a God who was separate, selective, jealous, and used tools of intimidation like judgement and exile. A God who reserved his love for those who served him.

This little detour regarding the characteristics of God is relevant because many of us connect to being made in the image and likeness of God. It's almost as if we unconsciously continued to follow suit. We encouraged and accepted an individualistic and ego-based approach to life while adopting an understanding of love that was limited to a select few who served us, pleased us, and loved us in return.

Rather than portraying a God with ego-driven qualities who loved like humans, what if we allowed God his true nature and then aimed to embody a divine love? A love that was not reserved for any exclusive group, saw no one as separate, judged no one unworthy, and had no regard for self-preservation at the expense of another? A fierce, firm, and fiery love that also carried an infinite well of empathy and compassion? A love that saw every nucleus of creation as an extension of itself, took nothing personally, and could not be offended? A love that saw beyond the narratives of our identities, circumstances, and actions to the innate soul of every human being? Souls that are simply trying to remember who they are and make their way home.

This embodiment of love dissolves any manifestation of fear because it understands that there is nothing to lose. We have nothing to lose except the opportunity to embody and become this love.

So what does all of this mean? What exactly does this embodiment of love look like in our daily lives?

We can begin by understanding that love does not see an individual on the surface or become consumed by the narratives surrounding them. Love understands that we have been shaped by our environment and are a product of our experiences; it sees the soul within an individual trying their best to navigate life. Love does not abandon someone because they do not embody the fullest version of themselves, meet society's expectations, or because they have done harm or acted immorally. Love will love someone despite their apparent shortcomings and support them in becoming the fullest version of themselves.

> Real love is also courageous, fierce, and willing to rock the boat and set the house on fire to facilitate transformation.

Essential to note, however, is that loving someone does not imply that we cannot communicate our disapproval, challenge them, or remove ourselves from a situation. Real love is also courageous, fierce, and willing to rock the boat and set the house on fire to facilitate transformation. To love someone is to encourage them to do and be better, even if they are resistant, and we might risk losing their friendship in the process. To love someone is to be willing to sacrifice our comforts, desires, and our pride for their well-being.

Throughout this book, we have reflected on various things, entertained alternative perspectives, and considered how it might all apply to our lives. We began by creating the space to redefine God and acknowledging all that surrounds the illusion of our individual identity. We looked at the relationship between hope and faith and their roles in our lives before taking a moment to understand the vibrations of love and fear. Then we took time to glimpse the power of our minds and expanded our perspective of breath. We met our narratives face to face, looked at the conveniences we place around accountability, considered our inauthenticity as corruption, and then acknowledged the impact of our conversations. We introduced a new perspective on gratitude, discovered our ability to work miracles, and tasted the medicine outside of time. That's when we created space to hear God's whisper over the noise of our mind, and now we reveal the wings of our love.

All these reflections are just some of the tools that assist us in embodying this extraordinary, indescribable force called love. Once we experience the world through the eyes of love, even for a moment, there is no turning back. We may lose our way from time to time and be overcome by the desires and limitations of our individual identities, but that love will always be calling us to return. It calls on us to acknowledge God in the eyes of every human being, in all of creation, and then to act accordingly. The commitment to embody this love is one we must consciously make again and again until it becomes all that we are. We are the only ones standing in our way.

THE WINGS OF LOVE

Chapter 15: Questions for You

◇ Can you recall moments when your love has been conditional and limited by your expectations and desires? How could you have expanded your love?

◇ Where can you make a more conscious effort to embody the wings of love?

◇ How and where can you allow the people in your life more freedom?

◇ Are there relationships in your life that call for forgiveness and can you see how someone's conditioning may have contributed to their actions?

◇ In your own words, what does it mean to love?

◇ What are some of the situations and places where you have a hard time seeing God? How can you shift your perspective and allow space for God to exist there?

CHAPTER 16

"Are you God?"

UNKNOWN CHILD

Are You God?

As the blue lights flashed and the siren sounded, I thought to myself, "Someone's in trouble, they better pull over." The lights kept flashing and the siren continued to scream. I couldn't understand why the culprit wouldn't just stop their vehicle already. I mean, this was the United States of America.

It wasn't long before it all made sense, and at nineteen years old, during my sophomore year at the University of Tampa, driving my brother's hand-me-down pick-up truck, I was going to jail. At least, that's how it felt when the cop forced me to pull over and then approached the driver's door with his hand on his firearm. I had seen episodes of *Cops* and knew this was not the somewhat lackadaisical law enforcement of Trinidad that I was accustomed to. There was no pleading my way out of this one with a promise to rectify the situation.

Luckily, it turned out to be a traffic violation, something to do with insurance or registration. I didn't go to jail, but I did receive a fine, a court date, and the gift of community service.

I had wanted to volunteer my time and energy for a while, so I didn't exactly consider community-service hours as punishment. This sentence was more like a nudge of encouragement to stop talking about it and follow through. Honestly, I wouldn't be surprised if I called that traffic violation into my life, because I was about to get way more than community service. I was about to get a wake-up call that would sit in the back of my memory like a treasure waiting to be rediscovered.

I chose to fulfil my community hours at an orphanage. I loved kids and figured it would be fun, easy, and a solid contribution of my time. After checking in with the administration, they directed me to wait in the playground and guided me through a doorway that transported me into a world of orchestrated chaos and excitement. There appeared to be hundreds of kids from ages three to twelve running, screaming, dodging balls, jumping rope, and wholly absorbed in their co-ordinated mayhem. The scene was intimidating, and I wasn't sure exactly how or where I would fit in.

On the distant edge of the playground, I saw some swing sets that appeared relatively quiet and figured it would be a great place to start. I tried to make my way across the courtyard discreetly so as not to attract much attention or get run over by a stampede.

That's when he spotted me, locked eyes, and ran full throttle in my direction.

I was convinced this kid must have been running to someone behind me, because I had never seen him before, and his excitement was palpable. I turned to look over my shoulder to confirm my suspicion, and that's when I felt this repeated tug on my jeans. He was fast. As I looked down, he stood there, bright-eyed, with dark-chocolate skin, and a smile that could have easily wrapped around his skull. He must have been about four or five, and his delight was infectious as he tugged at my pants while constantly jumping up and down.

I smiled warmly, a little taken aback, and tried to find the right words to greet my new friend. That's when he confidently looked straight through me and asked, with a calm excitement, "Are you God?"

I could feel my mouth open in an attempt to find words, but there were none. He stood there looking at me with a smile, awaiting my reply. I managed to get out, "N . . ." but before I could even complete my statement of denial, he laughed over it as if dismissing my response. Then he ran off and disappeared into a sea of play.

I looked everywhere for him during the following hours, but it was almost as if he had vanished, and I was left wondering if that interaction had ever really happened. I assumed he mistook my long-haired, bearded hippie-looking appearance for what we know as the typical depiction of a white Jesus.

That was all it was, I thought to myself. For years I never shared that story with anyone, because not only did it seem outrageous, but a tiny part of my ego was caught up in it. I mean, it's not every day that you are asked if you're God.

Over a decade passed before I shared that story with anyone. It wasn't that I intentionally avoided sharing it; I just quietly placed it in the closet of my mind and forgot it had ever even happened. You know, like when you receive a gift from someone, and you're not too sure what it is or how it works, you just smile, say, "Thank you," and put it aside until you have time to figure it out.

It wasn't until about fifteen years later, when I sat down to write a social media post about God, that it came rushing back as if it were the day before. I remembered his eyes, smile, and piercing words: "Are you God?" I recalled his outrageous laughter of dismissal over my response as if he had no interest in entertaining it. Then, of course, his disappearing act left no trace of his existence other than the magic dust he sprinkled at my feet.

However, as I relived the experience this time, it was so clear. That little boy wasn't asking me, at least not with a genuine interest in my response. It was a reminder. He left me with a riddle and knew I would one day figure it out. He uttered three of the most powerful words I would ever hear, and while everyone might interpret those words differently, he was saying, "Wake up, brother, God lives in you. Rise to your potential. We have work to do."

He came to remind me that I had to awaken to the God who lived within me before I could see God in everything and everyone else. While that little boy appeared to me many years ago with this message, it was also meant for you. That's precisely why you are holding this book right now.

GRATITUDE AND ACKNOWLEDGEMENTS

When we share energy or time with someone, we are no longer the same. We have been changed and they influence who we are from that moment on. I am eternally grateful for everyone who has crossed my path – from those who have shared a moment in time to those that have set up residence. They are alive in everything that comes through me. With that said, there are some individuals who have contributed directly to this manuscript either energetically, with their brilliance, or both.

To my family, thank you for moulding me, surrounding me with an unshakable love and allowing me the freedom to colour outside the lines.

Christian Hadeed, there are few who believe in me as much as you do. Your companionship, love and support for over thirty years has been unfailing. Jade Ammon, thank you for the mirror, for unconventional love, and for never leaving my side even when I insisted that you did. Kiana Hart, if it weren't for your love and encouragement during the first draft of this book, I don't think it would exist. I am forever grateful for you and pray that you'll always be close.

Jerry Besson, I was maybe twenty-four when you told me I would write a book one day, I believed you enough to at least try. The guidance and encouragement from yourself, Dominic, Alice, and the Paria

Publishing family has been instrumental in bringing this manuscript to completion.

Linda Sparrow, my time with you was exceptional. Thank you for the clarity you brought to my voice, vision and writing. Anu Lakhan, you hold some kind of editorial magic wand, but most of all your willingness to understand, allow me my voice, and commitment to protect me as a writer has never wavered. I am deeply indebted to you. To Judy Raymond, everything I heard pointed to an exceptional reputation. Thank you for the final touches and your willingness to take on this project. Laura Duffy, it said so much that you wanted to read this book before designing the cover; thank you for being invested and ready to change a few hearts. Rachel Valliere, you brought these pages to life with such elegance, I couldn't imagine anything more fitting. Thank you for being invested and your readiness to go beyond expectations. You made it clear this was not simply another design job. Amanda Smyth and Ira Mathur, having great writers and beautiful people at my side made this possible and you fit into both categories. Thank you for holding my hand.

Seane Corn, your guidance and support has had a significant impact on my life and personal evolution. It is a privilege to call you my teacher and friend. Thank you.

Bruno Hanson, you are an inspiration; thank you for allowing me to share your story. John and Andrew Hadad, thank you for countless inspiring and thought-provoking conversations. Pilar Pouchette, for your openness and trust. Ayana Leonard, thank you for your friendship, vulnerability and stellar cinematography. Damien Gurley, for always having my back and reading this manuscript twice before it even approached readiness.

Immense gratitude to all who are mentioned in this book: thank you for being in the right place at the right time,

To some of those who have been an ongoing support system

during the writing of this book or have contributed in subtle but valuable ways: Lau, Teresa Sabga, Lucinda Literary, Simon Lee, Troy Turi and Jolene Bayda, the Beyond Yoga and One Yoga communities, Muhammad Muwakil and Lou Lyons, Solman, the Full Bloom Family, Scott Sardinha, Che Lovelace, Andrew Laughlin, Ragaz, Domo, Damz and Sara, Reds, Stories Told By Sam, the Ammon family, Kristie and Johnny, Gregory, Attillah, Anthony Sabga, Anna Cadiz-Hadeed, and the Bahamian contingent.

To my closest, the people who surround me with ongoing unshakable love: you all know who you are, and whether I see you regularly or feel you from a distance, I love and appreciate you dearly. Thank you for excusing my absence and understanding my obsession with crafting this manuscript.

To you, the one holding this book, thank you for being born and all that you bring to this world. Thank you for your attention, your trust, and your desire and commitment to be a better human being.

Lastly, to God and all the names by which we call on Spirit, the God that lives within us all without exception: I am eternally yours and bow to you in honour and reverence. Thank you for holding me, seeing me, and helping me get myself out of the way so you could come through from time to time.

I love you all.

LOVE

ABOUT THE AUTHOR

Troy Hadeed believes the ultimate spiritual practice lives within our everyday relationships and that divinity exists in the heart of every individual. He has been practising and teaching yoga for over fifteen years, but has been questioning narratives, dissolving conditioning, and dissecting the human experience for far longer.

He lives on the north coast of Trinidad and Tobago, nestled in a community of trees and hummingbirds, but thrives on an active social life, introspection, and some interesting travel choices. When not teaching or writing, he can be found sharing insights through speaking engagements, coffee-shop conversations, and casual encounters in the most unexpected places.

Troy calls for us all to bring more intention to the way we live our lives and acknowledges that our actions, words, and even thoughts change the world. He hopes that if nothing else, his words and life help individuals reconnect to their understanding of God and aid humanity, including himself, in remembering what it means to love.

YOUR NAME IS **LOVE**
We're Family

Scan QR code below to...

◇ Join Troy's inner circle and stay up-to-date on what's happening

◇ Send Troy a message directly and share your thoughts

◇ Write a review for My Name Is Love (It would mean the world)

◇ Work with Troy one-on-one or join the online yoga family (30 days free)

◇ Put some faces to the beautiful people you met in this book and see some of the images surrounding their stories

◇ Support approved organizations and projects that change lives

◇ Share the love

https://troyhadeed.com/mynameislove-community/